Arms Control and Disarmament

Arms Control and Disarmament
The Critical Issues

JAMES E. DOUGHERTY

THE CENTER FOR STRATEGIC STUDIES
Georgetown University • Washington, D. C.
SPECIAL REPORT SERIES

The *Special Report Series* of The Center for Strategic Studies examines policy issues related to strategy. Each report is published under the guidance of a Center Steering Committee or Study Group which defines the scope of the study and assists in presenting the report. *Special Report Series* publications take different forms: background studies of crisis areas; examination of assumptions, problems, and research gaps related to United States policy; exploration of options which may confront policy makers. In each case the objective is to clarify and illuminate available choices without recommending specific policies.

THE CENTER FOR STRATEGIC STUDIES, GEORGETOWN UNIVERSITY, was established in September 1962 to study the elements and purposes of strategy in free and totalitarian societies. The term *strategy* is understood to include economic, scientific, military, psychological, and moral aspects. In its effort to provide a view of strategic problems as a whole the Center has two basic functions:

To inventory strategy-related research in university and research centers in the United States and in foreign countries, and to inventory study papers, testimony, and reports of the U. S. Congress. Location in the nation's capital aids the Center in serving scholars, commentators, and public policymakers throughout the free world by exchanging research products and materials, and referring inquiries to appropriate sources, scholars, and specialists.

To identify strategic issues as well as information and research gaps, and to initiate and encourage research efforts accordingly. This function includes publications, conferences, and specialized seminars which examine key problems from various viewpoints and allow a forum for debate and discussion.

PUBLICATIONS OF THE CENTER FOR STRATEGIC STUDIES

National Security: Political, Military, and Economic Strategies in the Decade Ahead, edited by David M. Abshire and Richard V. Allen, Hoover Institution Publications (New York: Praeger, 1963). 1072 pages. $10.00.

Soviet Nuclear Strategy: A Critical Appraisal, edited by Robert Dickson Crane (August 1963). 82 pages. $1.00.

Soviet Materials on Military Strategy: Inventory and Analysis for 1963, edited by Wlodzimierz Onacewicz and Robert Dickson Crane (January 1964). 140 pages. $2.00.

East-West Trade: Its Strategic Implications. Analysis and Inventory of Congressional Documents, 1959-1963. Samuel F. Clabaugh and Richard V. Allen (April 1964). 104 pages. $2.00.

Military Posture: Fourteen Issues before Congress, 1964. James H. McBride and John I. H. Eales (September 1964). 235 pages. $4.95.

Détente: Cold War Strategies in Transition, edited by Eleanor Lansing Dulles and Robert Dickson Crane (New York: Praeger, 1965). 318 pages. $5.95.

NATO in Quest of Cohesion, edited by Karl H. Cerny and Henry W. Briefs, Hoover Institution Publications (New York: Praeger, 1965). 492 pages. $8.00.

Latin America: Politics, Economics, and Hemispheric Security, edited by Norman A. Bailey, foreword by Eleanor Lansing Dulles (New York: Praeger Special Studies Series, 1965). 300 pages. $9.00.

PREFACE

The subject of arms control and disarmament is highly controversial and involves many problems with important policy implications. Whether to disarm, to what degree, and under what circumstances—these are questions of paramount importance to the Congress, to the executive branch, and to the public at large.

Opinions are sharply divided on these and other questions. The variety of solutions offered and the intensity with which they are advanced point to the need for defining the issues, the varying assumptions, and the basic problems.

Since The Center for Strategic Studies is initiating a report series on critical issues and problems, it seems appropriate to make arms control and disarmament the subject of the first report. The aims of this report are to identify basic issues, to discover research and information gaps, and to stimulate research and writing to fill those gaps. The Center hopes in this way to contribute to a better understanding of one of the compelling policy problems of our time.

The present report grew out of the Center's Arms Control and Disarmament inventory project established in June of 1965. To date the Center inventory consists of some 7000 entries on the literature of arms control and disarmament, the principal experts and organizations in the field, and current private and government-sponsored research projects. An additional report—on the policy process of arms control and disarmament—is now in preparation; a third report—on the economic implications of ACD—is being planned.

Arms Control and Disarmament: The Critical Issues was prepared under the guidance of a Center Steering Committee which helped establish both the dimensions of the problem and the organization of the materials and which evaluated the report prior to publication. The Steering Committee with Cornelius D. Sullivan as Chairman comprised the following: James E. Dougherty, Foreign Policy Research Institute, University of Pennsylvania; Vice Admiral Edward N. Parker (USN, Ret.), former Assistant Director, United States Arms Control and Disarmament Agency; David M. Abshire, Robert Dickson Crane, and Robert A. Kilmarx —all members of the Center's research group.

The draft manuscript was submitted to some sixty American and foreign experts for review and comment prior to publication. The experts were selected from the research, academic, business, and government communities and represent many divergent points of view on the subject. Their comments and criticisms were incorporated into the text whenever possible.

I want to express our appreciation to both the Steering Committee and the outside reviewers for their interest and to acknowledge the Center's debt to them for the constructive criticisms they offered.

ARLEIGH BURKE

CONTENTS

Arms Control and Disarmament

1. DISARMAMENT: THE PERSISTENT THEME

The Objectives of Disarmament

The debate over the best way for nations to seek their security in the face of military technology and its accompanying dangers is as old as civilization. The prophet Isaiah had a vision of swords being beaten into plowshares and of nations no longer being exercised to war. From ancient to modern times, in Western and non-Western cultures, philosophers have urged policies of restraint upon nations and statesmen, warning them not to rely too heavily upon arms and alliances, not to undertake war except as a tragic necessity and then only as a last resort and with a full assessment of its costs, and not to pass up any opportunity of pursuing peace, which the poet Dante called the greatest of all human goods.

Moralists, political theorists, and the classical writers of international law, especially in the Western tradition, have constantly warned that when governments have recourse to force in international relations to defend what they conceive to be their legitimate interests, they must comport themselves according to the canons of moral justice and political proportionality, as well as established legal norms. They have also insisted, increasingly since medieval times, that statesmen have an obligation not only to defend their own national interests but also to have a regard for the international "common good," and to strive to their utmost insofar as conditions will permit toward the construction of an international political community in which power will be controlled by, at the same time it supports, the rule of law.

The debate about the control, limitation, and elimination of arms has frequently preoccupied the world's diplomats in this century. It began at the turn of the century, when armaments races came to be looked upon as a major cause of international tension and war. It flared again during the deliberations of the Washington Naval Conference and the League of Nations Disarmament Conference, when statesmen gathered to discuss arms limitations and possible arms reductions. In the 1920s and 1930s, several Western governments were interested primarily in the idea of imposing ceilings on arms production, in order to save money by avoiding arms competition without adversely affecting the security of states, or else in proposing plans designed to reduce the particular military advantage enjoyed by a rival power.

The League of Nations and Disarmament

The rise of militant *anti-status-quo* ideologies and policies both in Europe and Asia made it impossible for the Western democratic states to move the League of Nations and all of its onetime members toward an unequivocal subscription to Norman Angell's thesis that war preparations, not to mention war itself, represent the height of futility from an economic standpoint. Meanwhile Maxim Litvinov, the delegate of the Soviet Union to the League Disarmament Conference, startled virtually everyone when he demanded the total dismantling of all armed forces and weapons, the elimination of all military budgets and military service systems, and the abolition of all military schools, training centers, war departments, and general staffs within a period of one year. Western diplomats looked upon Litvinov's proposals not as serious policy overtures but rather as devices of propaganda and political warfare—a cynical assault upon the Western concept of "collective security" diplomacy if not an outright affront to the political intelligence of European policymakers.

Although the League disarmament negotiations brought to light many interesting insights into the political and technical problems of reducing armaments levels—insights which were ignored for many years in the UN disarmament discussions *after* World War II—they did not lead to the kind of progress which might have served to preclude the outbreak of that conflict. In fact, the case can be made that the Western democracies' continued quest for disarmament in the 1930s while the Axis powers pursued a steady policy of arming helped to create an unstable international climate and to bring on World War II, which Churchill called "the unnecessary war."

U.S. Initiative—The Baruch Plan

The period since World War II has witnessed renewed efforts toward solutions to the greatly increased security problems of the nuclear age, in which the quantum leap in firepower represented by the A-bomb was soon multiplied by a factor of a thousand in the H-bomb, and subsequently matched by the quantum leap in delivery speed made possible by the ICBM. The earliest American disarmament proposal after World War II was in the form of the Baruch Plan, calling for the creation of an International Atomic Development Authority (IADA) within the framework of the United Nations. According to the Baruch Plan, which was based on the Acheson-Lilienthal Report, the IADA would conduct all "intrinsically dangerous activities" in the nuclear weapons field; own and control all sources of critical materials and related installations; carry on continuous research in nuclear weapons and all phases of atomic energy so that no state could ever surpass it in technical knowledge; license all national and private nuclear activities (such as peaceful atomic projects); approve the structure, design and capacity of all atomic installations; and reserve the right of inspection in any nation at any time without advance warning. The IADA was to be politically responsible to the Security Council and General Assembly of the United Nations, without being subject to any nation's veto power. It was to exercise exclusive control over all stockpiles of atomic weapons, which were to be distributed in such a way that a preponderant amount would never be available within the borders of a single nation. New projects for atomic development would also be located according to the same principle. If an aggressor seized the installations within his country, his move would supply a "signal" to the inspection system, and the facilities of the IADA would be placed at the disposal of the UN in sufficient time to enforce his compliance with international obligations under the threat of disaster.

The Baruch Plan was a bold and generous one for the United States to put forward at a time when the U.S. possessed the only A-bombs in the world. Some observers doubted that this country could actually follow through on the proposal if the Soviets should accept it. Many were puzzled by the Soviets' adamant refusal to accept the U.S. offer. Today, however, Western analysts are more inclined to think that it may have been unrealistic for the United States to expect Soviet acceptance of the Baruch Plan. In the Soviet view, the IADA would have been established largely on American terms for the simple reason that the United States, in virtue of its being far ahead of the USSR in nuclear technology, would be able to dominate the international control system to prevent its rival from obtaining independent ownership of nuclear weapons. During the course of the discussions, the Soviets accused the Western powers of trying to infringe the sovereign rights of the USSR, to establish international capitalist control over segments of its industry, to conduct espionage, and to perpetuate the Western nuclear monopoly—thus setting a pattern of argument that was to become all too familiar through future disarmament and arms control negotiations.

American and Soviet Proposals

Throughout the 1950s and early 1960s, Soviet and U.S. negotiators and statesmen met thousands of times, at different levels and places and in different bodies, to discuss various types of proposals with greater or lesser degrees of seriousness. At one time or another, they called for the following agreements: (a) a "ban" on all nuclear weapons; (b) conventional disarmament; (c) the creation of international police or peacekeeping forces; (d) a "cut-off" in the production of fissionable materials for weapons purposes; (e) a nuclear test ban, either partial or complete; (f) an "open skies" system of aerial inspection to prevent surprise attack; (g) the disengagement or reduction of forces in prescribed geographic zones, especially Central Europe; (h) the creation of "atom-free zones" in Europe and other regions of the world; (i) the liquidation of military bases on "foreign territory"; (j) the reduction of military budgets; (k) the demilitarization of outer space; and other kinds of formal armaments measures. Toward the end of the 1950s, interest began to shift from partial measures to comprehensive or total disarmament plans, as the Soviets presented their proposal for general and complete disarmament (GCD) in September 1959 and the United States submitted its blueprint for GCD "in a peaceful world" to the UN General Assembly two years later.

Disarmament without Controls—Controls without Disarmament

For many years, the debates were monotonously similar. The Soviets accused the Western powers of desiring control and inspection without disarmament. The Western powers reciprocated by accusing the Soviets of seeking a purely "declaratory disarmament" without adequate verification of compliance. The Soviets charged the West with trying to legalize espionage in the USSR under the guise of inspection. The Western allies in turn suspected that the Soviets were interested in disarmament negotiations primarily for the purpose of bringing about the dismantling of NATO and the severance of the military link between the United States and Western Europe. Nevertheless, international armaments negotiations became what Hedley Bull has called a "persistent theme" in the foreign policies of the leading powers.

Strategic analysts, particularly in the West, have devoted an increasing amount of attention to the problems of arms control and disarmament. Some Western analysts have been concerned that the West would be placed at a dangerous disadvantage if nuclear disarmament proceeded at a faster pace than conventional disarmament, because of the manpower superiorities presumed to be enjoyed by the Communist states, notably China. Other Western analysts have objected to the conduct of serious East-West arms talks before the NATO allies had worked out among themselves a satisfactory strategic concept for the local defense of Europe and for the sharing of nuclear decisions within NATO; there has been a definite fear in responsible Western quarters that the Soviets wish to exploit the disarmament theme in order to divide the allies. Still others within the West have been worried that substantial disarmament might lead to serious dislocations in the U.S. economy, possibly great enough to produce a recession within the Atlantic Community, despite American and United Nations studies of the potential economic impacts of disarmament which carried fairly optimistic assurances to the contrary.

Economic Considerations

Not a few Western intellectuals are convinced that the failure to make more rapid progress toward a genuinely disarmed world must be attributed largely to economic considerations. Citing the expectation that the cancellation of military contracts would have an adverse multiplier effect upon prices, employment, investment, and confidence in the health of the nation's economy, they are inclined to subscribe to the thesis that the "military-industrial complex" has a powerful vested interest in perpetuating the arms race and in strewing obstacles along the road to peace. The specific economic aspects of the disarmament problem will be dealt with in a subsequent report in this series. But the point to be made here at the outset is that, in terms of pure economics, the problems are soluble, and the American political system possesses the creative capabilities of solving them satisfactorily, if and when a significant degree of disarmament could be achieved.

Obstacles to Disarmament

For a fuller understanding of the arms impasse, however, it is necessary to look beyond economics. The essential difficulty does not arise out of the profiteering of certain individuals or groups, nor can it be eliminated by a purely economic motivation, based upon a vision of the many useful things which might be done both at home and abroad once military expenditures have been drastically reduced. The primary obstacles to disarmament, far from being economic, are political, strategic, and technical in nature. National military establishments are, historically, an intrinsic part of the international state system. They are deeply rooted in the characteristics of modern science and technology, of the global ideological-social-political competition, and of a world structure in which nation-states seem to be driven by a law of their nature to seek their security by engaging in some form of power accumulation and manipulation.

The Changing Situation

To conclude that the situation is entirely hopeless and that a catastrophic war is eventually inevitable is not warranted on the basis of the evidence. Changes have occurred within the Communist state system, even though the significance of these changes is by no means a matter of universal agreement. After many years of negotiation, a few modest arms control agreements have been concluded—the demilitarization of Antarctica; a partial nuclear test ban; the establishment of a "hot line" between Washington and Moscow to facilitate emergency communications; a UN resolution prohibiting the emplacement of weapons of mass destruction in outer space; and a mutually announced intention to cut back on the planned production of fissionable materials for nuclear weapons. The most important of these agreements, however, have been participated in only by the two superpowers, or by them and Britain, so far as the nuclear powers are concerned.* France and China have remained aloof from the arms control agreements of the 1960s. The outbreak of the Sino-Soviet dispute in recent years has, in the minds of many within the West, raised the chances of substantive Soviet-U.S. arms agreements. The Chinese nuclear detonations since October 1964 have made arms control—particularly a nonproliferation agreement and other closely related measures such as a comprehensive test ban treaty—appear more urgent than ever.

It must be admitted, however, that the international political environment of the 1960s has been far from conducive to disarmament and arms control agreements. Compared with the 1950s, the incidence of conflict in various sub-strategic forms has been, if anything, greater in this present decade. It is no longer necessary to point to Korea, Malaya, Indochina, Suez, Hungary, Quemoy and Matsu, or Lebanon, as indicators of international instability. Just since 1960 the world has witnessed a whole series of disorders—coups, civil wars, border incidents, conventional aggression, infiltration and subversion, social revolutions, national liberation guerrilla wars, "peoples' wars," interventions and hostile power confrontations—in many places: Algeria, Angola, Berlin, Congo, Cuba, Cyprus, Dominican Republic, along the Israeli-Arab borders, the Indo-China border, the Indo-Pakistani border, Kashmir, across the Straits between Malaysia and Indonesia, in Indonesia itself, in Kuwait, Laos, Rhodesia, Rwanda, Burundi, South Africa, Venezuela, Yemen and, of course, Vietnam. Many governments and other social groups have become uneasy. The international peacekeeping role of the United Nations has met with some serious rebuffs, and in

---

* The Partial Nuclear Test Ban Treaty has been signed by more than 100 states.

the most unstable areas regional organizations have not thus far been able to fill the bill. A new generation of potential "Nth" countries is beginning to debate publicly the decision whether or not to "go nuclear." Every year military technology becomes more complex and more difficult to bring under formal international control. An international environment which is characterized by rapid technological, social, and political change confronts those who must make ACD policy with grave dangers and grave responsibilities.

2. DISARMAMENT OR ARMS CONTROL? VIEWS ON THE QUESTION

Since World War II two distinct yet related approaches to the arms problem have predominated in American thought and policy planning: disarmament and arms control. In some respects the two approaches overlap and complement each other. In other respects they diverge from and compete with each other. Many analysts and policymakers have a foot in both camps, and would be reluctant to be categorized as belonging primarily to one group or the other. Nevertheless, there is a concept of "disarmament" which can be logically distinguished from "arms control," and there are two schools of thought, both in and out of government, which proceed from different basic premises, assign different orders of priority, and posit different objectives for the time frame in which policymakers must plan. Both are interested in peace and security, but their conceptions of the arms problem and how to deal with it are significantly at variance. Neither school of thought is willing to be incorporated into or reduced to the other. As a result, a certain amount of confusion has accompanied our thinking about long-range goals, short-term objectives, and specific policy emphases in current planning for international arms negotiations. This is perhaps understandable in view of the fact that ACD policy planning is a relatively recent phenomenon within the U.S. Government, even though no other governments have put as much effort into this work as our own government has since 1961.

The Disarmament Approach

On one side are those who believe that disarmament—that is, the substantial reduction or complete elimination of those weapons with which nations can commit aggression and wage war—must receive the highest and most urgent priority among all the objectives of our government. Most ardent advocates of disarmament are skeptical of the efforts of the United States Government to pursue national defense through a policy and strategy of continued deterrence at high arms levels. Some of them go so far as to contend that there are only two alternatives facing mankind: General and Complete Disarmament (GCD) or General Nuclear War (GNW). They deem it extremely dangerous to base policy upon the hope that several states might maintain nuclear arsenals for defensive and deterrent purposes for an indefinitely long period without setting off a holocaust. In their view, there is virtually a mathematical certainty that if stockpiles of nuclear weapons continue to exist, and if the process of proliferation to other nations is not checked by a general movement toward disarmament, these weapons will sooner or later be used in war—as if through the operation of some unavoidable law of necessity.

There is also the fear that once these weapons have been introduced into a conflict, the process of escalation to levels of unimaginable destructiveness may lie beyond human control. Hence, it is argued that the only way in which the United States can ultimately enhance its security is by getting rid of arms and inducing others to do likewise—not by developing or producing more arms. The advocates of disarmament, for the most part, are not opposed to short-term reliance upon a strategy of "minimum deterrence" as a preparatory step toward complete disarmament. They are usually inclined to regard with favor the Gromyko proposal for a "nuclear umbrella," to be retained by the two superpowers until the end of the third stage of disarmament. This form of deterrence is acceptable to them because it is intrinsically related to GCD, and hopefully brings it within reach.

Disarmament without Safeguards

At this point one ought to distinguish between the majority of the proponents of disarmament, who insist that disarmament must be mutual, reciprocal, effectively controlled, and so structured that it will not place any party at an unfair disadvantage, and a minority who regard the dangers of nuclear weapons as so grave that in their view the process of destroying arms is much more important than the safeguards accompanying such a process. The latter group would accept relatively loose inspection systems to police a disarmament agreement and would rely upon such vaguely defined factors as common interest, world opinion, fear of detection, unwillingness to return to the dangers of an arms race, and the economic and technical difficulties of circumventing an agreement on a substantial scale to deter nations from violating a general disarmament treaty.

Unilateral Disarmament

The most radical factions among the advocates of disarmament (including the "better red than dead" group) urges upon the government a policy of drastic unilateral action in this field. One type of unilateral disarmer, who is attracted to certain social-psychological theories of reciprocation in the rise and decline of human tensions, believes that if the United States takes a dramatic lead in dismantling its own implements of war, the Soviet Union and others may be induced to follow suit. Other unilateralists, however, are convinced that the United States should abandon its own military defenses, regardless of the prospects of emulation by other countries, because they think that this will reduce the world's available megatonnage by a sizable percentage, or that this will reduce the chances of GNW, or that a nuclear defense policy is intrinsically immoral and cannot be supported by any people that subscribes to humanitarianism or a religious ethic. In evaluating the suggestions of unilateralists, it is often difficult to determine whether they spring from altruism or from a sense of futility and fear of extinction. At any rate, it should be pointed out that the U.S. Plan for General and Complete Disarmament has nothing in common with the proposals of the radical unilateralists who comprise a minority of the disarmament school. Rather, the U.S. plan reflects the view of the majority that disarmament must be reciprocal, equitable, and safeguarded.

The Arms Control Approach

The arms control school is normally inclined to believe that general and complete disarmament lies beyond the world's reach at present for a number of complex strategic, political, and technical reasons which will be examined throughout this report. It is not unfair to say that the "pure arms controllers" consider GCD to be not only unattainable but also undesirable within the proximate future. This school is disposed to look upon the contemporary arms problem as a function of the existing system, deeply rooted in the essential characteristics of modern science and technology, the worldwide struggle of competing ideologies and political groupings, and an international structure in which nation-states have little choice but to seek their security through some form of power manipulation. Nevertheless, the arms controllers for the most part do not despair of the present situation. They do not see nuclear holocaust as the inescapable alternative of a failure to achieve GCD within the near future. In fact, they look upon such a line of reasoning as self-defeating because it leads to the dismal conclusion that since GCD is currently impossible, men must passively await the final nuclear cataclysm.

In the view of the arms controllers, it is possible to postpone Armageddon indefinitely provided that governments can be persuaded to pursue policies which are based on a realistic understanding of the actual political-military environment. So long as nation-states and dynamic political movements such as Communism depend upon armaments either for their security or for the accomplishment of their international objectives, governments must strive to manage power wisely and to safeguard the international environment against unintended war by minimizing the risks of technical accident, unauthorized use of nuclear weapons, strategic miscalculation, and other undesirable possibilities. Virtually all arms control proponents are agreed, too, that when military conflicts do occur, as is likely from time to time in an armed world, governments should use intelligence and restraint rather than engaging their military forces in operations which lead to uncontrolled escalation or to uninhibited violence and unlimited collateral damage to civilian populations. Most arms controllers support the quest for policies designed to induce all nation-states gradually to set aside the law of force in favor of the rule of law, and to build an international climate of mutual confidence in which peaceful cooperation will predominate over suspicion, hostility, and conflict, although as one might expect there are differences of opinion as to what this might mean in respect to the handling of specific critical problems of foreign policy.

The Scope of Arms Control

The term "arms control" is a comprehensive one and encompasses several ideas which may not be entirely compatible. In general, however, the concept of "arms control" implies some form of collaboration between adversary states, involving either formal agreement, tacit agreement, or unilateral action with a view toward reciprocation, in those areas of military policy which are conceived to be of common or coincident interest to the parties involved. In addition to the meanings outlined above the term refers to:

(1) efforts to prevent or retard the proliferation of nuclear weapons to nations not already in possession of them;

(2) a program of weapons research, development, and deployment, as well as strategic doctrine, which emphasizes the defensive,

nonprovocative aspects of national security postures, especially those associated with an invulnerable second-strike capability;

(3) holding quantitative rates of weapons production at or below those levels which a nation is economically and technically capable of sustaining so that other desirable social programs may be realized;

(4) prohibiting certain activities, such as nuclear testing in prescribed environments or the placing of weapons in orbit;

(5) improving facilities for emergency communications between adversaries, as in the Moscow-Washington hot line;

(6) cautious handling of crisis diplomacy with careful assessment of the implications and potential consequences of each move as exemplified in the Cuban missile crisis;

(7) regional tension-reducing arrangements, such as disengagement or "thinning out" of opposing military forces, and the creation of demilitarized or nuclear-free zones;

(8) a formal freeze on the production of fissionable materials for military purposes or on the production of strategic delivery vehicles, or an agreement to reduce the size of nuclear stockpiles or the numbers of strategic delivery vehicles to prescribed levels;

(9) efforts to separate nuclear forces and strategies from conventional forces and strategies by geography and command, by a "no first use" pledge or by time (through such a device as the "enforcement of a pause"). These are only some of the major concepts which can be classified under the heading of "arms control"; others could be added to the list. In brief, whereas the disarmament school believes that very substantial or total disarmament lies within the realm of feasibility within a relatively short span of time, the arms controllers are convinced that this lies beyond the "art of the possible" within the foreseeable future and that limited controls (which hopefully might set the stage for a gradual evolution toward a more peaceful world) are as much as we can or should seek within the years immediately ahead.

Disarmament and Arms Control

Naturally there is some overlapping in what the disarmers and the arms controllers advocate. Most of those in both groups, for example, supported the partial nuclear test ban treaty and the quest for ways to inhibit the uncontrolled proliferation of nuclear weapons technology. Most disarmers are in favor of arms control restraints, freezes, partial reductions, regional limitations, and other arrangements insofar as these lead to a diminution of international tensions and pave the way for more substantial disarmament either concurrently or at a later date. In other words, they see many arms control measures as a necessary prelude to or a part of the first stage of GCD. Nevertheless, many disarmers are suspicious of the philosophy underlying the arms control movement, because they think that its adherents, by and large, are not committed seriously to the eventual goal of total disarmament but are merely engaged in a self-deluding search for conditions that will permit the continued existence of national military establishments.

Disarmament versus Arms Control

The pure disarmers (as well as some arms controllers) are unmoved by talk of crisis management, stable deterrence, defense-emphasis postures, and city-avoidance strategies. Not a few disarmers fear that a little success in the field of arms control—with the hot line, the partial test ban, the prohibition against bombs in outer space, and a cutback in the U.S. production of fissionable materials—might be a dangerous thing, for it could lead to a relaxation of the sense of urgency over the arms problem and to a false sense of security.

Some of the more skeptical arms controllers, on the other hand, might be more eager to seek limited, verified arms agreements if they were sure that such agreements would not generate a misleading atmosphere of détente and build up international political pressures for efforts to "preserve momentum" in the "peace race" by devising ill-considered "next steps" toward GCD —steps which could conceivably disturb the existing strategic equilibrium, jeopardize the security of the United States and its allies, and finally bring on a nuclear war which might never have occurred if what they regard as the imprudent philosophy of total disarmament had been clearly rejected. These arms controllers wish to take certain steps to make the defense policies of the United States as rational as possible from the military and political perspectives, but they do not wish to undermine these defense policies by embarking upon what they consider the utopian road to GCD—a road which in their estimate could lead to disaster, not because a GCD treaty would be signed and later violated, but because GCD represents such a patent impossibility in the contemporary world that any government which attempts seriously to move toward it as an immediate policy goal is so mistaken in its approach to the arms problem that it is in danger of making crucial errors in the formulation of its national security policy.

Some arms control analysts hope that a prolonged application of a full spectrum of arms control policies might gradually produce a pattern of international political, socio-economic, technological, and military conditions which will permit a general tapering off of armaments competition and a substantial reduction of armaments levels, along with threats of surprise attack, infiltration, subversion, guerrilla warfare, and other sources of instability and insecurity. This change of pattern, of course, presupposes profound changes in the international state system, and the arms controllers who nourish such hopes are seldom sure that the hoped-for conditions can be brought about within any prescribed time span, e.g., by the year 1980 or 2000; some are more optimistic, others less, still others not at all.

Even the most optimistic arms controllers are usually reluctant to embrace the vision of a totally disarmed world which characterizes the radical disarmers. Whereas the latter are inclined to point to the dangers of keeping arms, the former often focus upon the dangers of trying to get rid of them, including on the one hand the instability associated with a rising tide of irregular conflict, and on the other the possible tyranny of a unitary world government.

One's preference for drastic disarmament or for arms control as the goal of national policy almost invariably arises from his philosophy of human nature and society, politics and international relations, especially his interpretation of the East-West conflict, and his preference for a particular military strategy. The more fully a person subscribes to an idealistic concept of man, and the more he is oriented toward a futuristic vision of the transformations that science can produce in the attitudes, emotions, and thoughts of men, the more likely he is to desire the early and complete elimination of national armaments and the readier he is to believe that the fundamental changes in the state system necessary to usher in GCD can be made through social engineering.

Members of the arms control school tend, on the whole, to be somewhat more conservative in their philosophical outlook. The more one is inclined, on the basis of historical evidence available, to accept the realistic interpretation of international relations and to shun the utopian approach to politics, the more likely he is to doubt that modern military technology can be banished by legal fiat, or that nation-states can, should, or will relinquish all of their own military power in favor of the United Nations, an international disarmament organization, or any other instrumentality of world government. Such an individual very probably believes that the chances of moving from an armed to a disarmed world under an adequate system of safeguards are extremely remote, and hence he will be interested in various modes of arms control as the best means of minimizing the risks of nuclear cataclysm and, at the same time, of enhancing the security of the United States and those allied countries which depend upon it for their continued independence.

Both the disarmament and arms control schools know divisions within their own ranks. Some advocates of disarmament seem to believe that the role of force in international affairs can be virtually abolished, or at least that all nuclear weapons can and should be exorcised from the face of the earth. Other proponents of disarmament think that it may be possible to remove nuclear weapons from the arsenals of states but that, for the purpose of deterring the nuclear rearmament of an aggressor at some future date, it will be necessary to deposit a monopoly of nuclear power in the hands of an effective international government. Until recently there was a widespread assumption among writers in the field that substantial disarmament must proceed concomitantly with the development of international peacekeeping machinery. In recent years this assumption has begun to break down as it has become increasingly apparent that the Soviet Union has no intention of allowing the peacekeeping mechanism of the United Nations to be strengthened on any basis except under the great-power veto. It is now sometimes suggested that progress in disarmament negotiations cannot be made contingent upon progress in the evolution of an international peacekeeping organization. Disarmament is held by some to be so imperative in our times that it must proceed independently of efforts to bring direct and indirect aggression under legal control.

Meanwhile, the proponents of arms control have had their disagreements over the form arms measures ought to take. Arms control measures may be embodied in formal agreements (e.g., a treaty) or in tacit, informal understanding. They might be carried out on a bilateral or multilateral basis or they might result from unilateral initiatives; * they might be clear and distinct, or uncertain and obscure. The concept of arms control embraces all those restraints that a nation consciously selects from a wide range of alternatives and freely imposes upon itself, in the management of its military forces, for purposes it deems rational and worthy. Arms controllers frequently disagree about the adoption of formally negotiated measures calculated to promote an international atmosphere of détente versus unilateral measures designed to improve the management control efficiency of the nation's armed forces in order to minimize the risks of

---

* Unilateral arms control initiatives in many cases should be distinguished from unilateral disarmament initiatives, especially where the former are designed to improve the flexibility, efficiency, and control of a nation's armed forces without in any way weakening the nation's military power.

technical accident, strategic miscalculation, premature escalation, and unlimited collateral damage in case of war.

In brief, some arms control measures may have the effect of reducing the total military power at the disposal of the United States, while others may have the effect of enhancing the flexibility of the general defense posture of the country, as well as its security. Arms controllers may occasionally see these as contradictory objectives. Frequently they differ as to whether the purpose of a specific arms measure should be to promote the atmosphere of détente between the Soviet Union and the United States, or to improve the position of the United States—either militarily (e.g., by freezing weapons technology when the U.S. holds a lead), or politically (e.g., by making policy adjustments designed to please the NATO allies).

Summation

The advocates of pure disarmament are impatient with the present condition known as "mutual deterrence," "armed peace," or the "balance of terror." In their eyes, the situation is so fraught with danger that governments must spare no efforts to achieve GCD as early as possible; some would accept certain risks in order to accomplish the objective, on the grounds that the risks of violation of a disarmament agreement are more manageable than the risks of deterrence failure. The arms controllers, by way of contrast, are more disposed to conclude that governments have only limited room for maneuver in the area of military security policies, and should devote their primary effort not to the less likely GCD, but to those measures—more likely to be within the reach of governments—which will help to create and maintain a stable military and political environment. A great many persons in the arms control group would by no means rule out general disarmament as the long-range objective toward which the international system is very slowly evolving, and which it might someday achieve in a genuine community of world-law-with-power, once the forces now making for social conflict have been transformed into something higher and beneficial to all mankind. But the arms control group draws a distinction between an ultimate goal which is held forth for inspirational purposes and a policy objective which requires immediate implementative steps.

3. THE UNITED STATES–SOVIET CONFRONTATION

The day may come when Soviets, British, Frenchmen, and Americans may perceive a common interest in maintaining a system of international order among the emerging societies. As the nuclear and strategic delivery capabilities of the Chinese Communists develop to the point where the latter can pose a credible threat to the physical security of the two superpowers, Soviet leaders might think that they have more in common with Western societies than with Chinese society; perhaps they have already begun to think so. In recent years, many Western observers have professed to discern in Soviet behavior a dampening of ardor for the cause of international revolution, an unwillingness to underwrite the militant policies of Peking, and a tendency to conduct diplomacy after the fashion of a status quo power. But until the situation changes markedly, the political-strategic confrontation between the United States and the Soviet Union will represent the area of greatest concern to American policymakers for the security of the United States. Although the "North-South" conflict between the developing and the industrialized nations, and the Sino-Soviet split, may be fraught with significance for the future, they are not now the immediate issue.

Several fundamental points about the United States-Soviet confrontation should be kept in mind. (1) At present the Soviet Union still seems more deeply committed in formal pronouncements to the promotion of anti-Western social revolutions and the support of wars of national liberation than it is to joining the Western powers in any effort to achieve stability in Asia, Africa, and Latin America. (2) Whatever degree of nuclear threat Communist China may pose to the United States in the

1970s—and this may be of sufficient magnitude to be a cause of considerable concern, as Defense Secretary McNamara pointed out to the North Atlantic Council in December 1965—nevertheless the Soviets, at present, pose the greatest potential military threat to the United States and will continue to do so for several years. (3) Although it may be possible for the two superpowers to communicate to each other certain tacit understandings concerning areas of coincident interest (such as the avoidance of a mutually destructive nuclear war, or the control of conflict between third parties, e.g., India and Pakistan), the United States and the Soviet Union continue to have more to argue about than to agree about.

Opposing International Political Objectives

The international political objectives of the United States and the Soviet Union are now and probably will continue to be fundamentally divergent: the kind of pluralist world order which the United States wants is incompatible with the type of Communist world order which the Soviet Union seeks. There are some who contend that the aversion of the Soviets to nuclear war demonstrates a peace-loving character which bodes well for the possibility that the two giants will be able to arrive at a mutually satisfactory political accommodation. But, despite the ambiguities that sometimes mark Soviet diplomatic behavior, for instance in the Vietnam conflict, U.S. policymakers are compelled to proceed on the assumption that the USSR is the only country in the world today wielding the power of decisions that could jeopardize the physical survival of the United States. What is more, the USSR is dedicated not only to altering the world distribution of power in its own favor but also to bringing about a change in the structure of society which involves the annihilation of Western social values.

One is entitled to ask, therefore, why the United States is engaged in formal negotiations over the arms problem with the

Soviet Union. How do disarmament and arms control talks, and the planning for them, fit into the overall strategic objectives of the United States? How are they related to the requirements of deterrence and defense? How are they supposed to contribute to the advancement of the national security of the United States? How do they dovetail with the exigencies of coalition diplomacy, especially in NATO? What kind of ACD policies would help the United States achieve its policy objectives and what kind would hinder it? These questions, admittedly, are not easy to answer. Unfortunately, they are seldom even asked in a sharp form. ACD is a relatively new field of analysis. It is filled with a welter of clashing voices, reflecting many different philosophical and political approaches to the arms problem. Most of the research and analysis to date have been focused upon narrow facets of the problem. The perspective of ACD within a systematic framework of broad national strategy has been ignored, relatively speaking.

It is perhaps inevitable that a philosophically heterogeneous democratic society will shy away from the formulation of what Liddell Hart calls "grand strategy." Such an effort invariably brings to the fore the conflicts of value on which divergent positions are based; hence the open society prefers to adopt a pragmatic approach to its policy problems. The closed society, on the other hand, can more readily formulate a coherent set of national objectives and a consistent strategy by which to pursue them, and enjoys the additional advantage of being less vulnerable to distracting political pressures from domestic groups whose concept of the national interest is incompatible with the current official version. This is not to imply that the Soviet strategic planners are infallibly wise, or that their arms control and disarmament policies are certain to promote their long-term objectives. In fact, the Soviets at times may be just as uncertain as we are in trying to assess the advantages and disadvantages of specific ACD measures. But once their policymakers have made up their minds, they can expect their decisions to be implemented in a more unified manner.

Soviet Arms Control and Disarmament Objectives

What are the Soviet objectives with respect to disarmament and arms control? Lenin taught that disarmament and pacifism are sentimental bourgeois dreams and that real disarmament could be achieved only with the destruction of the capitalist system. The question today is whether Soviet leaders, reacting to the dangers inherent in modern military technology, have significantly modified the revolutionary objectives inherited from Lenin in order to insure the survival of their own society. The Chinese Communist leaders have frequently accused the Soviets of deviating from Communist orthodoxy by seeking formal arms agreements with the bourgeoisie. Some Western analysts, noting the serious difficulties encountered by the Soviet economy in recent years, suggest that the problems of resource allocation have forced the Soviet leaders to become interested in slowing down the pace of military-technological competition. Others argue that the Soviets are interested in arms control agreements because they assume that a "plateau" has been reached in military technology and that no further decisive breakthroughs are to be expected in the "arms race." Still others contend that the USSR, concerned over China, is interested in using arms control and disarmament negotiations as a vehicle for mending its fences with the West.

All of the foregoing interpretations merit careful probing. Equally deserving of analysis in depth are the alternate not-so-benign possibilities that the Soviets are interested in disarmament and arms control as means of: (1) inducing the United States, over a period many years, to relax its efforts in the field of military research, development, and weapons production, thus suffering, as it were, a unilateral qualitative and quantitative disarmament in comparison with a non-relaxing USSR; (2) creating an international environment of ideas, attitudes and emotions which would make it safer for the Soviets to work out their imperialist ambitions; and (3) weakening and, if possible, bringing about the eventual disintegration of the United States worldwide system of alliances and forward positions and, in particular, undermining the chief military link between the United States and Europe—NATO.

Areas of Mutual Interest

In spite of these caveats, however, it is reasonable to assume that the Soviets share some arms control objectives with the United States. They are certainly interested in preventing accidental war (despite their occasional denials that there can be such a thing) and in minimizing the risks that local non-nuclear conflict will escalate unpredictably to an unwanted large-scale nuclear war. They may also be interested in preparations to limit collateral damage once general nuclear war should break out, but they do not admit or discuss such notions in public. They are probably interested in taking steps (not necessarily involving a formal treaty) to retard the proliferation of nuclear weapons to other countries which do not yet possess them. Since September 1963, the Soviets have shown themselves friendly to the idea of applying the control system of the International Atomic Energy Agency to large "atoms for peace" reactors donated by the nuclear states to the non-nuclear countries. Above all, they seem anxious to prevent West Germany from gaining access to the control of nuclear weapons, and they have exploited the fear of a nuclearized West Germany in their campaign against Western plans for nuclear sharing in NATO and against the U.S. draft non-proliferation treaty, but whether they seriously believe that the United States and Britain are actually trying to vest the FRG with the power of nuclear decision is highly doubtful.

As for freezes, production cut-offs or partial arms reductions in the strategic field, the Soviets are not likely to accept them so long as the United States enjoys any sizable margin of superiority. Nor are they likely to enter any agreement which involves either multinational inspection or "adversary inspection"—a concept which they appear no closer to accepting in practice today than they did ten or fifteen years ago. Throughout 1964 and 1965, both in the Eighteen Nation Disarmament Committee talks and in the UN Disarmament Commission debate, the Soviets called for a comprehensive nuclear test ban, but they insisted that it should be monitored by national detection capabilities, not by an international inspection.* Nevertheless, the Soviets will probably continue to look upon ACD negotiations as a useful channel for communicating with the Western powers, and for exerting influence upon the policies of the latter amid the tensions generated by more hostile confrontations, such as that in Vietnam.

The Nuclear Umbrella

Within recent years, there has been one interesting modification in the Soviets' negotiating position on general disarmament which a number of Western observers find moderately hopeful, not so much in its present meaning as in its potential implications for the future evolution of Soviet thinking in this field. This has been the proposal for the retention of the so-called "nuclear umbrella." Prior to 1962, the Soviets had always insisted that all military rockets must be eliminated in Stage I of the disarmament process. In September of that year, the Soviet Union submitted at Geneva a revised draft treaty, providing for "an agreed and strictly limited number of intercontinental missiles, anti-missile missiles and anti-aircraft missiles in the 'ground-to-air' category," to be retained by the two leading powers until the end of the second stage. A year later, Soviet Foreign Minister Andrei Gromyko informed the UN General Assembly that the USSR was willing to extend the notion of the "nuclear umbrella" as a guarantee against aggression until the end of the third stage of the disarmament process. On the surface at least, the Soviets

---

* They have also expressed interest in a threshold test ban treaty, provided that it be accompanied by a moratorium on underground tests below the threshold.

appeared to be moving toward what some American writers have called a "minimum deterrent" as a means of preventing strategic disequilibrium during the disarmament period. During the 1964 ENDC negotiations in Geneva, the Soviets refused to place any specification upon the number of weapons to be retained, except to say that the force should be minimal in quantity, before the Western powers had accepted the idea of the "nuclear umbrella" in principle.

Until they knew what they were being asked to commit themselves to, however, the Western powers were unwilling to make a commitment in principle. Indeed, apart from the question of numbers of weapons, there were other features of the Gromyko proposal which troubled Western negotiators. The stipulation that the United States and the USSR must retain the weapons "in their own territories" appeared to be clearly aimed at the U.S. Polaris missile force now deployed at sea; this force, which provides a high degree of strategic invulnerability to the Western deterrent through dispersal and mobility, would have to be dismantled in the first stage. Furthermore, under the Soviet plan, verification of vehicles retained would not begin until Stage II. In Stage I, the United States, while destroying its own missiles and verifying the destruction of Soviet missiles, would not be able to rely upon a system of international inspection in order to ascertain that the Soviets were not retaining a "nuclear umbrella" considerably larger than the one agreed upon. Finally, since the Gromyko proposal contained no modification of the Soviet draft treaty provisions demanding the liquidation of all foreign military bases during Stage I, it represented no basic change in the long-standing Soviet strategy of bringing about the dissolution of the NATO defense ties between the United States and Western Europe. The Soviets underscored this objective during the 1965 UN Disarmament Commission debates and the 1965 ENDC discussion in Geneva by reiterating their demand—in the context of partial next steps—for the liquidation of all overseas bases and the withdrawal of troops from foreign territories.

United States Arms Control and Disarmament Objectives

The United States in setting forth its outline for General and Complete Disarmament in a Peaceful World in September 1961 was motivated in large part by a desire to meet the propaganda challenge of the Soviets, who had presented their own plan for GCD to the United Nations General Assembly in September 1959. Some United States policymakers may have thought that GCD could actually be achieved within ten or fifteen years, but a growing majority has become convinced that GCD cannot be pursued by governments as a realistic policy goal under the political, strategic, and technological situation now prevailing in the world. Since 1963 especially, there has been a perceptible shift in U.S. planning away from GCD toward partial arms measures. A number of U.S. policymakers who were committed to the long-range goal of disarmament were disappointed by the Soviet effort to change the strategic balance by placing missiles in Cuba, and later by the adamant refusal of the Soviets to lend financial support to the development of peacekeeping machinery in the United Nations, despite a legal opinion from the World Court concerning their obligation to do so under the charter.

Limited Objectives

In the field of arms control the United States has been interested in accomplishing several objectives either through unilateral policy actions or bilateral negotiations. To prevent the accidental or unintended initiation of war, the United States has adopted a number of internal safeguards: e.g., the "failsafe system," which requires a positive Presidential order before SAC bombers on an alert mission can proceed beyond a prescribed geographic line; the "two-man rule," which requires the cooperation of at least two individuals for all operations connected with the handling, movement, arming, and firing of nuclear weapons; the "two-key system," which, in the case of U.S. nuclear weapons deployed on the territory of a foreign ally, would allow both the United States and the allied government to wield a veto over its use; and the "permissive action link," an electronic lock system which makes it physically impossible for commanders in the field to employ nuclear weapons without receiving a coded signal from higher authority, such as the Department of Defense.

The United States has developed such an elaborate system of political, administrative and technical safeguards over its nuclear weapons that some military authorities have expressed doubts as to whether the efficiency of certain types of responses might be impaired in cases where a rapid reaction is desired. In addition to these restraints the United States has also taken steps to construct an invulnerable second-strike capability (including command and control systems) to reduce the necessity for preemption. It has tried to reduce the dangers of uncontrolled escalation, especially in NATO Europe, by urging its allies to build up conventional forces, by withdrawing "soft" Jupiter and Thor missiles from forward bases in Turkey, Italy, and Britain, and by attempting to work out "rules of nuclear engagement" within the North Atlantic Council.

In the area of formal negotiations the United States has sought several arms control objectives since World War II. The unsuccessful attempt to induce the Soviets to participate in setting up an International Atomic Development Authority (under the Baruch Plan) to control all atomic energy activities has already been mentioned. Later, the U.S. effort to secure an "open skies" agreement to reduce reciprocal fears of a surprise attack proved similarly futile because the Soviets first rejected the proposal outright and subsequently linked it to a form of disengagement in Central Europe which was unacceptable to the United States. In 1959 the United States and the Soviet Union signed a treaty demilitarizing Antarctica; this was a gesture of more symbolic than strategic significance. In 1963 the two major powers concluded three arms control agreements: the "hot line"; the three-environments test ban; and the United Nations resolution banning weapons of mass destruction in space.

Over the five-year period from 1958 to 1963 the main U.S. motives in working toward a test ban had probably been (not necessarily in the order listed): to reduce the hazards of radio-active contamination of the atmosphere from fallout; to retard proliferation; to freeze what was taken to be a general U.S. superiority over the Soviets in strategic nuclear capabilities, particularly nuclear delivery systems; and to take a major "first step" toward formal arms control. Early in 1964 the United States and the Soviet Union issued simultaneous announcements—the former that it would decrease the production of fissionable materials and the latter that it would stop scheduled construction on two atomic reactors for the production of plutonium. Since January 1964 the United States has wished, among other things, to devise methods of obtaining a verified freeze on the production of strategic delivery vehicles, both offensive and defensive. The Soviets, however, have shown little interest in a freeze which, they declare, would entail the imposition of controls over Soviet missiles without any disarmament taking place.

During 1965 the United States devoted the major part of its efforts in the field of arms control diplomacy to negotiating an agreement that would retard the further spread of nuclear weapons. There was a question as to whether the proliferation of any segment of technology could be effectively inhibited by treaty. There was also a question as to whether a formal treaty was necessary to induce the two leading nuclear powers to abstain from aiding in the creation of other independent national nuclear forces, or whether, if this was a matter of mutual national interest, they could not be expected to pursue it tacitly. U.S. policymakers, however, finally decided that the world was in danger of moving into a condition of "nuclear anarchy," and that unless concerted action were taken soon the next decade might see more than a dozen additional states striving to enter the nuclear ranks. Hence in August 1965 the United States presented to the ENDC in Geneva a draft nonproliferation treaty whereby the existing nuclear states would promise not to take any steps leading to an increase in the total number of entities wielding independent control of nuclear weapons, while the non-nuclear states would promise not to manufacture or otherwise acquire such weapons. The U.S. draft posed complex political questions both within the NATO alliance and among several potential "Nuk" countries —questions which will be examined in the next section.

National Citizens Commission Recommendations

Late in 1965, a widely publicized report of the National Citizens Commission, Committee on Arms Control and Disarmament, issued in connection with the White House Conference on International Cooperation, recommended a number of steps to break through the current arms impasse. This report, which was not an official policy paper of any governmental agency but which set off several policy debates within the U.S. Government, called attention to a number of problems—the quickening trend toward "international anarchy," the dangers of a further round of competition in advanced weapons technology, the unresolved and volatile situation in Central Europe, the build-up of non-nuclear armaments in the developing areas of the world, and the question marks surrounding China's policies and her role in world affairs.

Shortly before the committee report was released, there had been two significant developments within the United Nations concerning the major Communist power in Asia. First, the UN General Assembly had rejected a bid to seat the Peking regime by a vote of 47 votes in favor, 47 opposed, and 20 abstentions. Second, the Political Committee of the United Nations, by a vote of 91 to 0, called for a World Disarmament Conference by 1967 in which the Chinese Communists would be invited to participate. The United States, without entering into an irrevocable commitment, indicated a willingness to take part "in a small initial group to explore areas of agreement for convening a world disarmament conference." In the mind of the well-informed observer there was an obvious connection between the prospects for the holding of the 1967 Conference and the future of events in Vietnam, in which the United States, the Soviet Union and Communist China were involved in an extremely complex strategic confrontation.

Perhaps the most controversial recommendation contained in the citizens' panel report was the one in which the United States and the Soviet Union were urged "to agree—explicitly or tacitly—to a moratorium of at least three years on new deployment (but not on the unverifiable research and development) of systems for ballistic-missile defense." The committee acknowledged that the current argument for ballistic-missile defense in the United States is that it would neutralize whatever limited threat might be posed by China in the 1970s, but nevertheless expressed doubt about both the military value and economic cost of the system, as well as its political implications, and suggested that a three-year moratorium would provide time for an assessment of the Chinese threat and of Soviet ACD intentions. The report reflected a five-year-old bias of a sizable segment of the U.S. arms control community against the anti-missile missile on the grounds that it is essentially "destabilizing," technically and practically impossible, prohibitively costly and, most recently, politically undesirable. The reason why the recommendation for the three-year moratorium is controversial, however, is that Soviet spokesmen have publicly rejected all of the principal Western arguments against defensive weapons and the Soviets appear to be proceeding, if not at a frantic at least at a steady pace, toward the acquisition of such a capability.

4. WORLDWIDE ATTITUDES ON ACD

ACD negotiations pertain primarily to the relations of the two superpowers, but they also intimately involve other powers, great and small. Obviously, the plans for GCD and for certain partial arms measures are fraught with profound implications for all the countries of the world. Plans for GCD could not be put completely into effect, or perhaps even substantially implemented, until they had been accepted by all states, either voluntarily or through coercion. Perhaps the time is passing, or has already passed, when the two superpowers could almost monopolize the international arms control dialogue. The year 1965 witnessed the emergence of several states which, like France, seemed to be increasingly aware that their own national interests in respect to arms control do not always coincide with those of the United States and the Soviet Union, even when the latter two are in agreement.

One can usefully think about the attitudes of the other powers in terms of the following categories: (a) the lesser nuclear powers; (b) the allies of the superpowers; (c) other potentially important states whose vital interests would be seriously affected by GCD or by specific arms control proposals; and (d) the smaller states, numbering about a hundred. All of these states wield some political influence upon the superpowers, either through "special relationships" such as Britain enjoys with the United States; through such alliances as NATO and the Warsaw Pact; through the pursuit of independent nuclear policies; through the threat of exacerbating local conflicts that might bring the superpowers into an unwanted direct confrontation; or through the negotiating mechanism of the Eighteen Nation Disarmament Committee and the debating mechanism of the 114-member United Nations Disarmament Commission.

The Lesser Nuclear Powers

France and China have refused to adhere to the partial test ban and do not participate in disarmament negotiations. It is a matter of debate as to whether either of these countries would be likely to adhere to a disarmament treaty or to an arms control agreement in the drafting of which they have not participated, although they may show more serious interest in formal negotiations in proportion as they advance in the technology of nuclear weapons and delivery systems. France under de Gaulle has up to now shared with the Soviet Union a contempt for the peace-keeping efforts of the United Nations.

As for Communist China the possibility of her participation in ACD negotiations is further complicated by the fact that she is not recognized by the United States and is not yet in the UN. Judging from Peking's stance with respect to Formosa, India's borders, and the war in Vietnam, as well as several statements that seem to suggest that she favors the spread of nuclear weapons to the emergent countries, China often seems bent upon demonstrating an ostentatious lack of interest in U.S. diplomatic recognition, in admission to the United Nations (except on her own terms), and in meaningful arms control agreements with the "capitalist states." But it cannot be predicted with any degree of certainty that China will deliberately promote nuclear proliferation, or shun all arms control arrangements, whether formal or tacitly understood.

Given her militant ideological posture, it would be difficult for China to enter into treaty arrangements with the West. Under no circumstances is she ready to subscribe to any test ban which would prevent the development of more sophisticated nuclear weapons, and she would probably be even more reluctant than the Soviet Union to accept international inspection on her territory for any arms agreement. She may be interested, however, in preventing the debasement of nuclear currency which would result from her giving aid to other aspiring "Nuk" countries.

Among the five nuclear powers, Britain has always seemed the most regretful of having ever got into the nuclear business in the first place and the most anxious to secure ACD agreements, probably because of her precarious geostrategic situation. Prior to its coming to power in October 1964, the Labour Party espoused plans to liquidate the independent British deterrent but since assuming a governing responsibility Prime Minister Wilson's ardor for denuclearizing Britain and setting an example for "Nth countries" appears to have cooled somewhat.

Britain has taken a strong lead in the effort to bring about an antiproliferation pact, but she has maintained a united front with the U.S. Department of State in insisting that a nonproliferation treaty should not foreclose the possibility of subsequently creating a NATO nuclear force. Her position in the ENDC talks during the summer of 1965, however, differed from that of the United States insofar as she insisted that either the United States or Britain always retain a veto against the future contingency of a European nuclear deterrent; she took exception to the language in the U.S. draft nonproliferation treaty which held open the theoretical option of a European collective force not subject to either an English or an American veto.

In the meantime the British government has become increasingly concerned about the defense of the country's strategic interest "East of Suez" (e.g., in Kuwait and Malaysia). This concern, along with the present political impasse over nuclear sharing in NATO, has probably given rise to second thoughts in Britain over the abandonment of nuclear forces. Another trend worth close attention is the growing cooperation between Britain and France in the realm of technology. If Britain, largely for economic reasons, should someday prove willing to enter an *entente nucléaire* with France as the price of admission to the Common Market, then the gap between the British and French positions on at least some aspects of ACD policy might narrow.

The Warsaw Pact Members

With respect to the attitudes of the allies of the two super-powers, little need be said of the policies of the Warsaw Pact members. Apart from Poland none of the East European Communist states has become identified with any original initiatives in the ACD field. Poland, because of its geographic location and also because of the still unsettled matter of Germany's eastern territories, has deemed it advantageous to advance the Rapacki-Gomulka plan for denuclearization, or at least a nuclear freeze in Central Europe, instead of a complete military disengagement of NATO and Warsaw Pact forces. The Rapacki-Gomulka plans have, of course, been advanced with the approval of Moscow. All the East European members of ENDC (Poland, Czechoslovakia, Rumania, and Bulgaria) take ACD positions so closely aligned to that of the USSR as to be indistinguishable from the latter.

At present the East European states possess no nuclear weapons and there is a general consensus that the Soviets have not deployed a substantial nuclear capability in East Europe. From time to time it is suggested that if the United States creates a nuclear force for the Atlantic alliance the Soviets may have little choice but to admit their Warsaw Pact partners to a share in the control of nuclear weapons. It is not at all clear, however, that the pressures for nuclear sharing within the two European alliance systems are comparable, since the two alliances themselves are politically quite nonsymmetrical. There is no doubt that some of the East European states—especially East Germany, Czechoslovakia, Poland, and perhaps Hungary—are economically and technologically capable of producing their own atomic devices. Certainly the Soviets would never permit them to do so. Whether the Communist regimes in those states would have any motives for trying to acquire nuclear weapons is a question that has scarcely yet been examined by Western analysts.

West Germany and NATO

Within NATO, although it is the complex of interalliance relationships involving France that is the focal point of present difficulties, it is the question of Germany which causes the greatest long-range concern. U.S. policymakers, realizing the importance of preserving German confidence in the American defense commitment, have sought ways of strengthening a NATO that has been foundering on the issue of nuclear weapons control without doing anything that could be construed as proliferation. If West Germany should lose faith in NATO as the guarantor of her security, the moderate politics which have characterized the history of the Federal Republic in the Adenauer-Erhard era may ultimately give way to political extremism, polarized between a desire to seek a national nuclear force as a bargaining counter for reunification and a willingness to accept total demilitarization and neutralization as the price for rejoining what the Communists call "the two Germanies."

The West Germans have publicly asserted that so long as the Federal Republic's security can be underwritten by a collective deterrent or its equivalent they will have no need to acquire their own atomic forces. In the meantime West German spokesmen have argued that the FRG is the only state in the world which has already renounced, in an international treaty (i.e., the Paris Agreements of 1954) the invention and manufacture of nuclear weapons, and should not be required to undertake new treaty obligations before other states have taken the preliminary steps already taken by the FRG.

The MLF and the ANF

The proposed multilateral nuclear force and its British counterpart, the Atlantic nuclear force, were perhaps ill-conceived mechanisms for strengthening NATO. Many Western critics have contended that an MLF or its equivalent would add little militarily to NATO, and that it would not in the final analysis prove politically satisfying to those allies, especially West Germany, that wish to share in the control of NATO's nuclear strategy, if the United States retains a veto. President de Gaulle, moreover, has opposed the creation of the MLF, not because he fears that it would place nuclear weapons in the hands of the Germans (as the Soviets charge), but because it would run counter to his own conception of NATO and of French objectives in Europe.

The Soviets, seizing upon the dilemmas facing the United States, have attempted to extract the permanent renunciation of the MLF and the ANF as a concession for further progress on a nonproliferation agreement, and thereby to sow the seeds of distrust between the FRG and its premier ally. The Europeans themselves might eventually move, with or without encouragement and aid from the United States, toward some form of joint European nuclear deterrent. It is not at all certain that the major European states could be induced to sign any nonproliferation treaty which would preclude such an option. The U.S. Department of State was interested throughout 1965 in allaying West German misgivings to the effect that the concept of nuclear sharing within NATO was about to be entirely subordinated to the principle of nonproliferation as a guide to U.S. foreign policy. The Department of State realized that the erosion of the solidarity of the Atlantic alliance, and the cutting adrift of Germany, might have long-range consequences for the international strategic equilibrium no less grave than the process of nuclear proliferation.

Potential Nuclear Powers

Several other countries figure prominently in the ACD picture. Arms experts have made various estimates that a number of states beyond the existing nuclear powers and other states mentioned above—including Belgium, Canada, India, Israel, Italy, Japan, Sweden, and Switzerland—are capable of producing atomic weapons during the next decade. Still other states, such as Australia, Pakistan, Indonesia, and the UAR, would have powerful motives to acquire nuclear weapons in one way or another either for defensive or expansionist purposes. If China's international prestige is significantly augmented as a result of her atomic tests the Indian government will be under strong pressure to "go nuclear." Pakistan, concerned over the Kashmir dispute with India, might either seek nuclear weapons or move toward an alliance with China. Eventually Japan might wish to reestablish her status as a leading power in Asia by traveling the nuclear path. Indonesia publicly announced her nuclear ambitions prior to the crisis of September 1965, and if she should at a later date move far to the left and again pursue an expansionist policy, Australia would probably look to the English-speaking states for nuclear assistance. In the Middle East, Israel and the UAR have long been engaged in armaments competition. In Europe a great many Swedes and Swiss are reluctant to forfeit the possibility of acquiring nuclear means to protect their "armed neutrality."

Western arms controllers are adept at formulating cogent theoretical reasons why "Nth countries" would be unwise to seek entry into the nuclear club. A small nuclear arsenal, they argue, does not constitute a real power; the effort to build a deterrent might have a ruinous effect on a nation's economy, and a nation with bombs but no advanced delivery systems runs high risks for dubious political and military advantages. Nevertheless, since the United States became a nuclear power four other states have safely passed through the period of initial acquisition when vulnerability to preemptive action is highest, thereby demonstrating to other aspirants that the mere acquisition of nuclear weapons is not in itself a *casus belli* and is not likely to become one.

Security Guarantees for Non-Nuclear States

The proponents of a nonproliferation treaty have pressed for guarantees against aggression to be given by the nuclear to the non-nuclear states. Many difficult questions, however, remain to be answered. Would these guarantees be given by all the nuclear states collectively, or by some of the nuclear states, jointly or unilaterally? Would they be extended to all non-nuclear states, or only to certain important ones which feel themselves especially exposed, such as India? Is it conceivable that the Soviet Union, China, and the United States would jointly guarantee India's integrity, or that a Soviet commitment against potential Chinese aggression would have any meaning? Would the guarantee involve a conventional or a nuclear response in case a nuclear power commits aggression against a nuclear abstainer? Would the guarantee come into play against any attack or only a nuclear attack? Is it likely that any country which could manufacture its own nuclear weapons would prefer to rest its security upon the promise of an outside power or powers with which it has perhaps never been previously allied? Finally, is the United States prepared to undertake, with respect to many non-Western states or perhaps all the states of the world, mutual defense obligations which may be similar to or even stronger than those undertaken in Article 5 of the North Atlantic Treaty with respect to the countries of Western Europe? Difficult questions such as these prompted several analysts and some diplomats to question the wisdom of trying to develop a system of guarantees in connection with a nonproliferation treaty.

During 1965, both in the United Nations Disarmament Commission and in the Eighteen Nation Disarmament Committee in Geneva, the neutral non-nuclear states showed themselves somewhat reluctant to sign the kind of draft nonproliferation treaty put forth by the United States. They questioned whether this was an appropriate "next step." India and Sweden took the position that the effort to reach a nonproliferation agreement seemed to be discriminatory against the nuclear "have-nots" inasmuch as it placed no unpleasant burdens upon the present nuclear powers. Several neutral states preferred that the "next steps" should take the form of such measures as a comprehensive nuclear test ban treaty, a freeze on the production of fissionable materials for military purposes, and initial moves toward the reduction of existing nuclear weapons stockpiles. The neutrals did not look favorably upon U.S. efforts to impose International Atomic Energy Agency controls upon "atoms-for-peace" reactors in the developing states while most U.S. reactors and all Soviet, Chinese, and French reactors remained outside the scope of IAEA controls. In sum, the neutrals seemed unwilling to commit themselves to the concept of nonproliferation until they felt more certain that the five nuclear states seriously intended to start moving in the direction of nuclear disarmament among themselves.

Consideration of the foregoing issues leads to the conclusion that generalizations about the attitudes of the states of the world must be avoided, and so must simplified formulas to be applied equally to all states, large and small, committed and uncommitted, industrially advanced and underdeveloped. Not a few "middle powers" when they think of disarmament think almost exclusively in terms of the relations between the two superpowers, not of the implications of disarmament for their own defense and foreign policies. Many undeveloped states hope, not always realistically, that disarmament would release massive resources for international development aid, but their diplomats and leaders often lack a comprehensive grasp of the complexities inherent to the arms problem. There is scarcely a state in the world today willing to accept *for itself* the full political consequences of drastic disarmament, including the development of effective institutions of international government to whose decisions it would be willing to defer in matters touching upon its vital national interests.

5. MILITARY SECURITY AND ACD

The Problems of Evaluating ACD Proposals

In evaluating the military security implications of ACD proposals it is necessary to distinguish between GCD proposals and partial arms control measures. Although it is difficult to predict precisely what effect any arms measure will have upon a nation's total defense posture, it is much easier for a government to evaluate a specific carefully drawn proposal for a single step designed to modify the nation's military posture than for it to weigh the long-range significance of plans that involve total disarmament. Governmental bureaucracies are usually conservative, cautious, and slow-acting when it comes to changes that affect national security. They examine and reexamine a single proposal for months or years, assessing all of the predictable implications before offering it or accepting it.*

Not infrequently a proposal which at first glance looks attractive will upon closer scrutiny arouse grave suspicions as to its merits. A responsible government, say the advocates of partial measures, may under certain conditions be willing to run moderate and limited-liability risks, but they will not consciously embark upon the radical transformation of the international strategic environment which is implicit in all plans for GCD. If confidence is to be built up between hostile states, say the arms controllers, this can be accomplished only by slow degrees through partial measures, not by visionary proposals which, if accepted, would profoundly disturb the power relationship with which states are now familiar.

---

* This is the usual practice; a good example of which can be seen in the five years of test ban negotiations which preceded the partial test ban treaty.

In contrast, the advocates of GCD contend that partial measures lead nowhere for the following reasons:

(1) Governments are fond of proposing partial steps, but reluctant to take them because it is almost impossible to conceive of specific arms moves which would really lead to symmetrical improvements in the security situation of each side. Each nation has a unique geostrategic situation (size, shape, location, approaches, borders to be defended, concentration of population and industry, interest to be upheld, etc.) and an arsenal of various types and quantities of weapons tailored to its own needs; hence it is difficult to design alterations in military postures which will appear equal to both sides, although it is possible that a satisfactory equality might emerge from prolonged bargaining.

(2) The effects of specific arms measures cannot be readily calculated because governments do not know where they will lead in a world that remains armed. If, for example, there should be an agreement to destroy "obsolete bombers" (U.S. B-47s and Soviet TU-16s) this might merely serve to free economic resources for the subsequent development of other weapons systems.

(3) Each nation fears that the other nation, in proposing a partial measure, is either seeking a one-sided military advantage (as in Madariaga's famous allegory of the animals' disarmament conference), or else is trying to score an international propaganda victory for a decision to cut a certain military program or weapons system—a decision previously taken for military, economic, technical, or other reasons that have relatively little to do with the objective of disarmament. Therefore, conclude the partisans of GCD, the only remedy for the deficiencies of the partial measures approach is for states to commit themselves to the abolition of all "externally oriented armaments" within a relatively short period of time. Only then do all unilateral assets and liabilities cancel out, only then can security be assured. GCD is thus supposed to be commended by its neatness, its thoroughness, and its simplicity.

The fact remains, however, that the achievement of GCD would have to consist of a complex series of partial steps, and the arguments which the total disarmers often adduce against partial measures can also be applied against the various steps to be undertaken in the initial phase of GCD. The U.S. draft outline of a GCD treaty submitted in April 1962 provided for a 30 per cent reduction of military forces in Stage I, which presumably would take at least three or four years to accomplish. A number of military experts would probably be willing to agree to such a reduction, provided it would be accompanied by the necessary degree of verification, even if it did not seem likely that the conditions for proceeding with Stage II would be realized. But even in Stage I, there is still the complex problem of where to begin the process of disarmament. The McCloy-Zorin statement of September 1961 contained the principle that disarmament should be carried out in such a way as not to place either side at an unfair military disadvantage. That, of course, is a sound principle, but the two superpowers have been arguing ever since about what it means and how it should be applied, especially in the crucial Stage I.

Planning for ACD—Some Problems

A number of difficult questions arise in connection with the planning for disarmament or arms control.

1. *On what intelligence estimates of the existing military situation do the policymakers base the formula for reducing armaments levels, redeploying weapons, or slowing down the rate of military-technological development, whether qualitative or quantitative?* This is important especially in those cases where different intelligence organizations have different estimates of the present situation, or of the situation which will obtain at a given time if present trends continue as projected or if they are modified in prescribed ways. Without highly reliable and accurate intelligence concerning where the nation stands militarily in relation to the capabilities of its potential opponent, including, e.g., precise knowledge of weapons—numbers, types, ranges, yields, protection,

location, performance characteristics, state of readiness, and the kinds of command, control, and communications systems to which they are subject—it is not possible to engage in genuinely scientific planning for disarmament and arms control. Similar problems confront decision makers in a period of military-technological competition which is not characterized by formal arms control agreements, but these problems become more serious to the extent that governments really intend to move toward substantially lower armaments levels.

2. *How fast and how far down the scale should the United States go in reducing armaments?* In the case of ICBMs, for example, should it be willing to go down to a verified parity with the Soviets (whether expressed in the number of comparable vehicles, or in total deliverable megatonnage, or in some other way), or should it insist upon a reduction to some agreed fraction of the strategic levels presumed to exist at the time the agreement is made? There has been a good deal of discussion within recent years about the possibility of exchanging maximum for minimum deterrence by working toward a strategic situation in which the United States and the Soviet Union would eventually maintain not the hundreds of ICBMs which they are capable of producing and deploying, but a much smaller number, say 50 or 100 well protected missiles, sufficient to deter the other from launching a first strike through the threat of "unacceptable damage" in retaliation. This agreement would be less convincing, of course, in the case of a rationed force of from 500 to 1000 missiles. (The latter figure, however, would hardly represent a reduction, since it is probably larger than the 1965 Soviet ICBM force by a factor of perhaps three.)

Some people who want a freeze on nuclear strategic delivery vehicles seem to have a minimum deterrent in mind as an eventual goal, or as an intermediate phase along the road to GCD. The Soviet proposal for a "nuclear umbrella," a strictly limited number of missiles to be retained by the two superpowers on their own territory until the completion of Stage III of GCD, is comparable in a way to the notion of a minimum deterrent and was put forth as a "concession" to the West. As pointed out previously, however, the Soviet plan involves features which make it absolutely unacceptable from the standpoint of U.S. and European security. Others who advocate a freeze on strategic delivery vehicles do not view it as a move downward to a minimal deterrent, but as a means of prolonging a U.S. strategic advantage which might very well erode if the Soviets continue to build ICBMs and gradually achieve "saturation parity."

Unfortunately there is no rational basis for the belief that as the level of strategic armaments keeps dropping, the safety of the international environment against the outbreak of war necessarily improves commensurately. To eliminate on both sides portions of quantitatively large nuclear missile forces would serve to reduce the extent of urban-industrial damage in case war occurs, but there is probably a point (never to be defined with certitude) beneath which it would be extremely dangerous to reduce the size of nuclear forces, for this would raise the incentive to cheat on an arms agreement in order to carry out a successful surprise attack. It is more profitable to cheat at low levels than at high levels of strategic arms, easier to alter the ratios of power in being rapidly, and easier to knock out a substantial portion of an adversary's stationary forces. Moreover, it is virtually impossible to arrive at a satisfactory definition of what constitutes "unacceptable damage" to an adversary whose value system is radically different from one's own, although Defense Secretary Robert McNamara has attempted to do this within flexible limits.

In fact, it is impossible to get the experts to agree among themselves as to where the line lies which separates "military stability" from "military instability." The problem of defining military balance is greatly compounded by the intervention of political and psychological factors which elude the grasp of the quantifiers. Logically, the notion of "stable balance" implies some parity of countervailing forces. But this does not hold true where the complex dynamics of international politics are concerned.

In a situation of perfect mathematical equality in respect to military forces, one side might still prevail over the other if it boasts a stronger "psychostrategic" constitution and is less afraid to brandish its power in close support of its policy, especially at times of crisis. Conversely, a viable balance can be struck when one side possesses a surplus of military forces over the other, provided that the preponderant party happens to be—by virtue of its ethical tradition, its psychological and ideological attitude, its political-diplomatic style, and its military doctrine—in a defensive position and needs the power surplus in order to carry out its global defense obligations against a potential imperialist movement, which usually enjoys the advantage of being able to choose the time, place, and method of applying outward pressure.

3. *To what extent is there a danger that a series of partial arms control measures combined with an atmosphere of détente will have an adverse cumulative effect upon the U.S. research and development effort before it has been unequivocally established that the Soviets are seriously interested in arms control?* Perhaps no single measure can be shown to jeopardize the national security, but several measures related to nuclear testing, to budgets, to military systems in space, to the further development of bombers and missiles, and to the development of antimissile defenses, might place military R & D under various subtle restraints and eventually downgrade the effectiveness of the U.S. deterrent. A vague politically inspired presumption that the arms race is leveling off is no substitute for an assurance based upon adequate verification that both sides are simultaneously slowing down their programs of advanced weapons technology.

It is especially important that U.S. arms policy be based upon hard knowledge, and not merely optimistic guesses, concerning Soviet activities in space military systems, qualitative improvements in missiles, and the development of ballistic missile defenses. Up to the present time, U.S. arms control planners have avoided including R & D in U.S. arms control proposals. The Wiesner Report of November 1965, produced by a panel of the National Citizens Commission referred to previously, wisely excluded R & D from its proposed three-year moratorium on the deployment of ballistic missile defense. Until such time as it is clear from several years experience that the Soviet Union is equally interested with the United States in a permanent turning down of the military-technological contest through verified arms agreements, the United States has no chance but to strive for leadership in advanced weapons technology.

4. *What are the dangers that, after disarmament has proceeded to an advanced stage, one major power should scrap the agreement and suddenly pursue a policy of remobilization,* perhaps with the intention of exploiting the advantages of hidden stockpiles of atomic, biological, and chemical weapons that should have been, but were not, turned over to the International Disarmament Organization? How long would it take for the democratic states of the world to realize that a potential aggressor was actually reversing the movement toward disarmament? How much longer would it take the democracies to realize the magnitude of the challenge posed to their security? How glaring a violation would there have to be before they were brought to the point of abrogating an agreement into which they had solemnly entered? Would they be galvanized into an immediate reaction or would they engage in an enervating debate about proof that a violation had occurred or about the nature of the sanctions to be applied? What sort of effective sanctions could be applied, short of the immediate remobilization of the democratic states themselves? Would a centrally planned economic system such as that of the Soviet Union be able to carry out in secret elaborate bureaucratic preparations for remobilization so that the pluralist societies would not be able to make an appropriate defensive response in time, regardless of how rapidly they reacted?

To those who are sincerely concerned about the dangers which the continued existence of massive nuclear stockpiles pose to mankind, and to the security of the American people, the very posing of such questions as these may seem to constitute a form of rhetorical sniping at the disarmament movement. Nevertheless before substantial progress can be made on the road to disarmament, it will be necessary to supply realistic answers to these questions, and credible safeguards against the risks which they imply.

6. TECHNICAL PROBLEMS OF ACD

Monitoring Military-Technical Activities

The technical problems of disarmament and arms control arise primarily out of the nature of modern military technology, which is characterized by rapid and incessant change, as well as by remarkable variety. The main question is whether the regulation or prohibition of military-technological activities, whether by means of informal, tacit moves—"reciprocal measures," as U.S. arms control writers call them or, to use the Soviet term, "mutual example"—or by means of written instruments which have been formally negotiated in accordance with the processes of traditional diplomacy, can be effectively "monitored," "inspected," or "verified." The term "monitoring" usually refers to national intelligence-gathering activities; the terms "policing" and "inspecting" refer to the work of formal international control organizations; the term "verifying" encompasses both national intelligence activities and international inspection. International inspection might be carried out by a multimembership control organization or simply by adversaries—i.e., if the USSR and the United States should enter an agreement limiting the number of missiles, they could police it merely by inspecting each other, whereas a more ambitious scheme for world disarmament would certainly require a control organization with personnel drawn from all, nearly all, or many states.

Virtually all ACD agreements, with only a few obvious exceptions, such as a "hot line," involve requirements for unilateral intelligence-gathering by the U.S. Government to monitor compliance by other parties. Unilateral intelligence activities and international inspection can usefully supplement each other, when both are available. The U.S. Government would prefer both in most cases, although there may be certain types of arms control agreements (such as those which lend themselves to policing by satellite reconnaissance) for which it may be possible to rely upon military intelligence alone, and to abandon the demand for formal on-site inspection. Generally speaking, the availability of intelligence depends upon the ingenuity of a government's agencies and the effectiveness of other governments' counterintelligence efforts; the availability of inspection depends upon the willingness of the various parties to grant access to inspectors.

Up to now, there have been no formal disarmament agreements, and it is presumed that the United States will not enter any formal disarmament agreement which fails to provide for international inspection or, perhaps better still, mutual adversary inspection. Thus far there have been four formal arms control agreements entered into by the USSR and the United States— the demilitarization of Antarctica; the partial test ban; the "hot line"; the ban on bombs in orbit—and one informal one (the mutual declaration of intent to cut back on the planned or scheduled production of fissionable materials). None of these arms control agreements contained any provisions for international inspection, although the Antarctica treaty permits inspection by national teams,* and inspection is irrelevant in the case of the "hot line."

Apparently the U.S. Government is satisfied that it possesses an adequate capability to monitor the other agreements for itself and to be prepared to make an appropriate response if it becomes aware of a failure to comply on the part of the Soviets.** As other arms control agreements are entered into, it will probably be necessary for the United States to regularize the process of

---

* The United States conducted its inspection of the stations of six of the signatory powers, including the Soviet Union, in January 1964. This is not the same, however, as inspecting an installation on Soviet territory.

** Senator Henry M. Jackson has raised a question as to whether the Soviets have cut back or increased their production of fissionable materials since the spring of 1964.

monitoring the agreements and of keeping the Congress informed concerning the manner in which previous agreements are being observed.

Technical-Administrative Problems

This general problem of verification in the broadest sense appears to be the most intricate of all the technical problems associated with disarmament and arms control. Quite properly, it has been the object of much study within the United States since the mid-1950s. There are several other technical-administrative problems, but most of them are related either directly or indirectly to the subject of verification and to the type of international control mechanism that the signatory parties would be willing to accept. Before taking up the central issue of inspection, it may be useful to pose some of these related questions:

1. *Must the powers stop arming before they start disarming?* It would seem to be a matter of simple logic that the states of the world would not undertake to dismantle existing weapons systems until they are reasonably certain that other states are not continuing the production of similar weapons to replace those destroyed or instituting the production of new and unfamiliar weapons which may not even be covered by the disarmament agreement. Nevertheless a great deal of modern disarmament thinking is based upon the assumption that the most urgent task is to begin destroying existing weapons and that controls on the production of other weapons can be progressively instituted as disarmament proceeds and nears completion. It is quite conceivable, however, that if the disarmament were phased out over several years, say five to ten or more, and if the rights of full access were denied to inspectorates until all weapons inventories declared at the start of disarmament had been eliminated, another very large and formidable arsenal of the most up-to-date armaments might have been produced during the era of old-weapons disarmament, ready to be deployed quickly for a first-strike while

the non-cheating party was trying frantically to make a defense-production response. This is why the United States has always steadfastly refused to consider disarmament plans, such as those advanced by the Soviet Union, under which inspection is limited to "declared armaments and facilities"—i.e., those in the actual process of being dismantled—while full access to look anywhere for weapons retained or produced in violation of the agreement is withheld until the disarmament process has been completed.

U.S. arms control and disarmament planners must keep in mind the possibilities of clandestine production during the disarmament period when they evaluate the effectiveness of such concepts as "progressive inspection," "non-obtrusive inspection," "zonal inspection," "graduated access inspection," and other partial inspection methods. Inasmuch as the most vital considerations of national survival are at stake, no effort should be spared to make certain that U.S. policymakers have a complete understanding, based upon the most careful scientific study, of the need to insist upon disarmament agreements under which the production of new weapons is reliably precluded more rapidly than old weapons are destroyed.

2. *In planning to verify formal arms agreements, how should U.S. policymakers relate intelligence-gathering activities with inspection?* Some advocates of ACD, in their desire to reach agreement with the Soviets, occasionally argue that if the United States can depend upon existing intelligence capabilities in a certain sector, then it can afford to relax its demands for highly reliable inspection systems. But this might prove unwise and troublesome in the long run. The best intelligence estimates are, more often than not, imprecise. They can seldom be proven and frequently lead to erroneous conclusions concerning situations which affect the security of the United States.

Furthermore, over a period of time, intelligence capabilities change: they might either improve or disappear altogether in a specific geographic or functional area. Inspection systems furnish additional guarantees against this contingency. Inspection ought to be kept at a sufficiently high level of intensity that any violation of an agreement which adversely affects the security of the

United States can plausibly be detected by and attributed to the formal inspecting organization, even where the original lead might be furnished by intelligence personnel; in this way, intelligence sources can be protected. Hence intelligence needs and inspection needs should be analyzed independently of each other. Intelligence should not be regarded in U.S. arms control and disarmament planning as a substitute for high-reliability inspection.

But the existence of intelligence capabilities furnishes the United States with an important additional safeguard, beyond formal inspection. In certain situations where multimembership inspectorates have become lethargic, infiltrated, corrupted, or intellectually and scientifically inferior—developments to which all bureaucratic institutions are sooner or later prone—unilateral national intelligence activities may mark the difference between survival and annihilation. For this reason, international arms agreements, whenever possible, might contain realistically drawn "escape clauses," similar to Article 3 of the Partial Test Ban Treaty, which permits a signatory party to withdraw whenever *extraordinary events* related to the subject matter of the agreement affect the national interest, without having to submit any legalistic proof of violation on anyone's part. The withdrawal clause feature was also included in the U.S. draft nonproliferation treaty submitted to the ENDC in August 1965.

3. *Can military technology be controlled by written agreements?* Agreements are made up of words, while weapons are made up of physical substances; words and weapons are quite different things. When an effort is made to circumscribe the sovereign prerogatives of governments, whatever is forbidden or limited must be meticulously defined so that governments may not evade the agreement by doing what is prohibited under the guise of what is permitted. In the drafting of any agreement concerning the numbers of offensive and defensive strategic delivery vehicles, for example, there would be a serious problem of distinguishing between forbidden military ICBM production and permitted production of rockets for the peaceful exploration of space, or between military and commercial jet aircraft of intercontinental range. Moreover, despite the fact that such terms as "strategic

nuclear weapons" and "tactical nuclear weapons" appear over and over again in contemporary ACD literature, and sometimes in the Geneva arms discussions, such terms are unsuited to formal international arms agreements. Language must be precise; weapons must be described in detail. Hence when the United States offered its proposal for a verified freeze on strategic delivery vehicles during 1964, U.S. negotiators defined "strategic delivery vehicles" as missiles and bombers of an exact minimum gross weight and striking range.

Paradoxically, the more precise the language of a treaty is, the more easily at times can the architects of military technology circumvent it. Even while the diplomats spend months or years hammering out their treaty clauses word by word, scientists and engineers may be rendering their literary draftsmanship obsolete by devising new types of weaponry. Thus does incessant and unpredictable change in military technology prove to be the bane of many legally structured arms agreements and control systems. Experienced negotiators will agree that it is extremely difficult to draft a prohibitory clause in such a way as to rule out lengthy arguments a few years later as to whether or not a specific type of production or activity constitutes a violation of the treaty.

4. *In the case of substantial or complete disarmament, what should be the structure and functions of the international control organization?* A number of political, legal, and administrative issues arise in connection with the international organization which would be created to police an agreement for substantial disarmament. These issues are by no means insoluble. But they are intricate and warrant careful study. Many of them were debated during the years 1958 to 1963 when efforts were under way to devise an international control organization to monitor a comprehensive test ban. Not every arms control agreement requires an elaborate organizational structure to ensure compliance. But a verified freeze on strategic delivery vehicles, or a reduction of nuclear weapons stockpiles, or a general cut in the arms levels of all states, would probably revive the relevance of many of the following questions.

Who would the members of the control organization be—all

states or only some? Would all members have equal powers? What would be the legal status and political authority of the control organization? Would there be a single administrator and a control commission? How would they be selected? What would be their relationship to each other? How would the control organization be financed? How would its headquarters be staffed? How many monitoring stations would the control organization maintain on the territory of the various states? What would be the number and nationality of the staff needed to man each monitoring station? Who would determine the exact location of the monitoring stations? Over what types of questions would national governments retain vetoes with respect to the operations of the international control organization within their own territories? What would be the procedures for determining that violations of the disarmament agreement had occurred? How much right of access would the personnel of the international control organization have within the boundaries of each state? Would it be the same for all states, or vary from state to state? What techniques of inspection would be employed? What kinds of technical equipment would the control organization maintain for the performance of its mission? Would the control organization have military force at its disposal, and if so, what kind? To what body would the control organization be responsible, and how would the responsibility be enforced?

The answers to all these questions, of course, depend upon one's assumptions as to what a disarming and a disarmed world would look like, and how states would probably behave in such an environment. This brings us back to some of the points which were raised early in the memorandum in connection with the various philosophical approaches to international relations and to the armaments problem.

7. PROBLEMS OF VERIFICATION

Requirements of an Inspection System

Although a voluminous body of theoretical literature has been produced on the subjects of verification and inspection, it is important to remember that up to now the nations of the world have had relatively little practical experience in operating international inspection and control systems. Various arrangements for the control of fissile materials have been studied by such organizations as the International Atomic Energy Agency, Euratom, the European Nuclear Energy Agency of the Organization for Economic Cooperation and Development, and the Armaments Control Agency of the Western European Union. These organizations can furnish useful insights into the requirements of effective inspection systems but they themselves have had only limited success, because of political obstacles, in incorporating known requirements into their own operations.

During recent years, many useful analyses of inspection and control problems have been completed by governmental agencies, the military services, scientific organizations, private research institutes associated with universities and industry, and individual analysts throughout the country. Nevertheless, it is still almost impossible to obtain a consensus among the experts on the precise requirements for an inspection system needed to monitor a specific disarmament or arms control measure.

The experts are fairly well agreed that it is impossible to design a single technical system for international control and inspection which would work for all types of agreements. The type of system needed varies according to the specific objective.

It depends upon what is being regulated, and the extent to which it is being regulated. Indeed, for each particular disarmament or arms control agreement, it might be possible to select among alternative control systems, combining different mixes of the many techniques of verification which are theoretically conceivable. Moreover, the experts concede that no single inspection technique is foolproof; ways can be devised of avoiding detection no matter which inspection method is applied. But, they argue, the reliability of the inspection system can be increased by crossing several techniques and by applying scientific sampling methods.

A control organization can inspect for many different things; fiscal-administrative support for arms programs; weapons research and development activities; weapons testing; personnel involved in armaments program; procurement of critical materials; the manufacture of arms; the transportation of critical materials or armaments; the stockpiling of weapons; the training of personnel for the handling and use of weapons; the deployment and maintenance of weapons systems at ready locations.

Actual inspection methods may include the following: supervision of the destruction and transfer to international control of nuclear weapons; supervision of the dismantling of military installations and the mustering out of forces; supervised close-out of declared production facilities; measurement and analysis of known productive plants; surveillance of industrial plants and plant records; strict accountability of critical materials; surveys of manpower and skilled labor shifts; stationing of permanent inspectors at sensitive production plants; random on-site inspection of nonsensitive factories and other installations of suspected military potential; stationing of permanent or temporary observers at key transportation centers to observe traffic; controlling the chemical processing of irradiated materials; registration and surveillance of scientific and engineering personnel; detection of radioactivity from tests and waste disposal; aerial and outer space reconnaissance; monitoring of governmental budgets and accounts; inspection by the people; and psychological inspection.

Problems of Nuclear Weapons Control

While many analysts agree that it lies within the technical state of the arts to devise a moderately reliable system of controls against future clandestine production of nuclear materials and strategic delivery vehicles and the deployment of such weapons to secret launching sites *after the control system has become operational,* no authoritative writers in this field deny the impossibility of constructing a physical inspection scheme which would preclude the danger of nuclear weapons caches being diverted from stockpiles built up prior to the disarmament agreement. Such weapons might be subsequently used to carry out an aggressive attack with commercial jet aircraft quickly converted to bomb-carrying purposes.

At present the margins of error which might inhere in U.S. estimates of the Soviet Union's total previous production of fissionable materials could be sufficiently great to pose the issue of national disaster for the United States if a treaty for general and complete disarmament should be concluded and implemented within the foreseeable future, because there is no known scientific method of physical inspection that can certainly uncover clandestine stockpiles, whereas the "non-physical" inspection methods which have been suggested theoretically (i.e., inspection by the people and psychological inspection), besides being politically unacceptable, are still unreliable from a scientific standpoint.

Problems of Biological and Chemical Weapons Control

Heretofore, the great bulk of ACD studies within the United States have been addressed to the problem of controlling nuclear weapons. *Less* attention has been paid to the question of biological and chemical (B/C) weapons control, and those who have studied the subject are virtually unanimous in concluding that, irrespective of how intricate the task of controlling nuclear weapons might be, the job of policing an agreement prohibiting the production and stockpiling of B/C weapons would be considerably more difficult. It is true that the military effectiveness of these weapons is a matter of some controversy among military specialists themselves, some of whom point to their fragility, uncontrollability, and unpredictability under certain conditions. Nevertheless, in a world in which nuclear and conventional armaments were being reduced, B/C weapons might become more interesting to potential aggressors.

Programs of R & D in this field can be carried on with smaller budgets, fewer scientists and technicians, less conspicuous facilities, and fewer critical materials. Nearly every chemical factory, agricultural experimentation center, and hospital or university biological laboratory is a potential site for research of military utility. During the years that GCD negotiations would be in progress, fully equipped and supplied research labs might be constructed underground in remote areas, with practically no chance of being discovered by inspectors for several years. Many types of B/C weapons can be handled and transported much more easily than nuclear weapons, and in a disarmed world they could be delivered by a great variety of means: weather balloons, commercial aircraft, ships, pellets dropped in water supplies, and so on. Field testing sites could be readily detected, but governments may soon know enough about a great number of biological and chemical agents, lethal and non-lethal, to dispense with testing.

One of the principal dangers associated with this category of weapons is that they lend themselves to slow, hard-to-detect deployment and even to gradual ambiguous forms of use which create doubts in the minds of the victims as to whether they are under deliberate attack or suffering the effects of natural phenomena. Hence, because of all these complexities, even some advocates of GCD, although intensely interested in nuclear disarmament, are not sure that B/C disarmament is a feasible objective. The U.S. plan for GCD cautiously calls only for studies in Stage I, to be followed by steps in Stage II which are deemed appropriate in the light of the studies made.

Verification as a Political Problem

In the final analysis, the task of verifying compliance with a specific disarmament or arms control agreement is not merely a technical problem. It is also in a very real sense a political problem. Theoreticians can play on paper the game of "hiders and finders" and come up with all sorts of hypothetical computations regarding the kind of inspection system needed to police a specific agreement with a prescribed percentage of reliability. But if a major power is politically unwilling to accept the level of intrusion which the theoretical model presupposes for its validity, then the hypothetical model turns out to be of little practical use. Even if a state accepts a certain inspection in principle it can dilute its effectiveness by interposing subtle political obstacles—modifying a significant function or power of the control authority, changing the composition of a headquarters staff, vetoing an operation here, denying access there until it is too late for the inspectorate to uncover evidence, arguing technicalities, causing delays and doing other things to skew the results which the games theorists expect to derive from purely random sampling activity.

Much of the discussion about inspection within recent years has been carried on in a political vacuum. Even within an open, democratic society such as the United States, inspection for substantial disarmament would raise knotty constitutional, legal, and political problems since it would entail the invasion of private and corporate rights. In a country like the USSR—with its strategic secrecy complex, its neurotic suspicion of comparison with the outside world, and the fear of its leaders that high levels of inspection would introduce alien influences and undermine totalitarian control—it is less likely that any given inspection system would be politically tolerable. One should not forget that up to the present time the Soviets have presented no concrete evidence that they are willing to accept international inspection in practice. There will be no such evidence until an international inspection has actually been carried out in an unimpeded manner on Soviet territory.

8. THE BALANCE SHEET

The Possibility of General Nuclear War

Most analysts of the contemporary strategic scene seem to believe that the United States and the Soviet Union now share a rather strong motivating interest in the avoidance of general nuclear war or of any war which involves strikes against the other's homeland. According to this view, the two superpowers have gradually moved, either consciously or unconsciously, toward the development between themselves of an understanding that they will not engage in a mutually annihilative nuclear exchange. This is an assumption rather than a prediction. Naturally, it is impossible to say with certainty that nuclear hostilities will never break out between the United States and the Soviet Union. Although it is difficult for Western policymakers at the present time to conceive of any sudden technological breakthrough which might tempt the Soviet leaders to embark upon a path of "nuclear adventurism," such a possibility cannot be entirely discounted; there is no assurance that the Soviets—confident that "socialist technology" is supreme—have abandoned the hope that they might surpass the United States in advanced weapons technology. Nevertheless, the most common interpretation of the present situation is that the Soviet Union and the United States, despite their sharp disagreement over such problems as the war in Vietnam, discern a significant coincident interest in limiting their adversary relationship so that it remains below the threshold of nuclear war, or even any direct military embroilment with each other.

GCD and Security

Limiting their adversary relationship does not mean, however, that the two superpowers look to general and complete disarmament as the only way or the best way of safeguarding their security within the foreseeable future. Neither of them has acted within recent years as if it believes that GCD is really essential, or that it represents a feasible policy goal to be pursued at the present time. Indeed, at least four of the five existing nuclear powers—with Britain as the only possible exception, and even this is debatable—appear to attach a higher priority to policy objectives other than general disarmament under conditions which would be mutually satisfactory to all five.

Both the United States and the Soviet Union have submitted for international negotiation proposals for total disarmament which cannot be seriously negotiated in a world which is still ideologically divided, in which the policies and strategies of nation-states have become more rather than less complex as the result of technological developments, and in which the future of international peacekeeping institutions remains in doubt. There are some observers who think that the United States may have been unwise when it ventured into the arena of utopian diplomacy in September 1961 with its proposal for "general and complete disarmament in a peaceful world." In fairness to the architects of that plan, it should be pointed out that the U.S. proposal did serve to break the Soviet monopolistic claim to a special concern over the problems of peace and disarmament.

The Soviet Union has consistently refused to accept the Western demands for thorough inspection of disarmament and for the development of effective peacekeeping machinery. They have continued to propound the simplistic ideas that the mere destruction of weapons will solve the world's problems, and that "complete" controls need not be instituted until after "complete" disarmament has been carried out.

During the debates of recent years, within the United Nations and at Geneva, the diplomats of several non-nuclear states have been educated in some of the complexities of the arms problem, and they are now better able to understand what the United States has been advocating with respect to disarmament throughout the postwar period. All of these results are on the credit side. On the debit side of the ledger, however, it should be pointed out that the emphasis that the United States placed upon general disarmament in its public diplomacy during the early 1960s led to a certain amount of confusion among the American people, many American intellectuals and opinion-molders, some European allies, and perhaps even a few U.S. policymakers, with respect to the general direction and objectives of this country's ACD policies.

Possibilities for Progress in ACD

The fact that total disarmament does not now represent a practical political and technical possibility should not be taken to imply that no progress can be made in the area of arms control and arms limitations. Since 1963 both the United States and the Soviet Union have demonstrated an interest in using most of the time available for arms negotiations in order to discuss those partial measures which have some chance of issuing in agreement. This interest reflects an assumption that, while the two powers will probably continue to carry on their military-technological competition, they may also find it to their mutual interest on occasion to accept carefully defined arms control arrangements, or to communicate to one another understandings of a less formalized nature.

The ENDC furnishes an appropriate channel through which the two powers, while arguing about formal proposals, are able to exchange views on problems of security and on at least some military and political aspects of their national strategic policies. Each government tells the other at least a part of what it is thinking—what it would like to do if it could, what it feels obliged to do, and what it is concerned about in the political and military policies of the other. The dialogue is not a completely frank one, but virtually everyone agrees that the dialogue is both useful and beneficial, inasmuch as even a distorted communication is usually preferable to no communication at all.

Measures Worth Pursuing

Measures which genuinely reduce the possibilities of war by accident, strategic miscalculation, or uncontrolled escalation of limited conflict will always be worth pursuing. This is primarily a matter of efficient management of military power. More can probably be accomplished in this area through unilateral decisions based upon intelligent military planning, combined with tacit communication, than through efforts to arrive at formal diplomatic agreements. There may also be times when both sides find it to their advantage to formulate policies of military restraint which involve the redeployment of forces, or reductions in the size of available forces, or modifications in weapons development and production, provided that the moves which are made on both sides are genuinely reciprocal. At other times, each party can be expected to use ACD negotiations to score debating points, or to cause political embarrassment to its rival, or, if possible, to secure a unilateral military advantage over the other. For both sides the subject of arms control must always be intimately related to considerations of national security and military policy. Specific arms control proposals will inevitably be judged within this larger context.

Proliferation

At the beginning of 1966, the major question in the minds of arms control analysts was whether any effective steps could be taken to forestall the further proliferation of nuclear weapons to states other than those already possessing them. The majority opinion in the field seemed to be that an increase in the number of nuclear states would be likely to lead to an increase in international instability, insofar as the chances of accident, miscalculation, or deliberate nuclear aggression would thereby be greater. Not all analysts subscribed to this hypothesis, however. Some were convinced that the most important factor was not the mere *number* of nuclear states, but the *quality* of the policies pursued by the governments of nuclear powers.

There was a question as to whether the spread of nuclear weapons could be prevented by the conclusion of a nonproliferation treaty under which governments would declare their intention to abstain from certain policies without creating an international mechanism to verify compliance by all signatories. There was also a question as to whether, even if a nonproliferation treaty could not be agreed upon, the five existing nuclear powers would nevertheless find it to their interest to refrain from assisting other states in the effort to acquire nuclear weapons. France and China might not wish to dilute their own prestige by fostering the nuclear aspirations of other states and yet at the same time they might have compelling political reasons for refusing to enter into a formal treaty pledge.

The nonproliferation issue was linked to several knotty problems. It was intimately involved with a whole complex of diplomatic dilemmas within the Atlantic alliance and with the Soviet effort to compound NATO's difficulties. It was also related to the attitudes of the neutral non-nuclear states, many of which shied away from the idea of a nonproliferation treaty until the existing nuclear powers, including China, would give credible evidence that they were making progress toward nuclear disarmament. But such progress, in turn, is hinged upon the willingness of the Communist states to accept international control as an essential concomitant of substantial arms reductions; upon the ability of the Western states, the Communist states, and the neutral states to reach a satisfactory compromise on the future evolution of effective international peacekeeping machinery; and upon a settlement of the conflict in southeast Asia which would augur well for the development of conditions conducive to more peaceful change.

There was reason to fear that if the strategy of "national liberation war" (or "peoples' war") should triumph in Asia, this would usher in a period of heightened international instability and conflict. The methods of the more militant advocates of international Communist revolution would have been vindicated; several weaker states would then be faced with risks to their security; the dangers of widening conflict and war would grow. Conversely, there was reason to hope that if the United States and its allies could turn back the latest, and in some respects the most serious, form of Communist aggression to date, the prospects would grow brighter for a period of enhanced stability in which the governments of the world—including China—would have an opportunity to take a very serious look at the problems of armaments and national security and, putting aside polemics and utopian proposals, strive to make realistic progress toward their solution.

ARMS CONTROL AND DISARMAMENT TERMINOLOGY

The problem of terms and their meanings, common to all areas of public policy, is particularly acute in the arms control and disarmament field. The reasons for this are many, but the following are among the most important:

a. Arms control as understood today is a new field, its vocabulary is fluid, its scope difficult to define, and its relationship to other fields not fully developed.

b. Technological advances related to the field of arms control and disarmament are dynamic. They provide new systems and means to be controlled, new monitoring devices and techniques, and new prospects for violations of agreements.

c. Various individuals and institutions within the public and private sector tend to use terms in different contexts to reflect their own particular point of view.

d. An international language for arms control and disarmament is lacking. There is no internationally accepted arms control vocabulary.

e. The language of arms control and disarmament relates more to aspirations, plans, and proposals than to experience. It lacks concrete referents in many instances.

Lack of agreement about the meaning of a number of important terms such as inspection and verification could give rise to treaty loopholes, unintended violations of the letter or the spirit of understandings, and, in some cases, to opportunities for deliberate cheating. Such possibilities could occur in spite of the most careful efforts of international lawyers and diplomats responsible for drafting agreements.

The more significant arms control and disarmament terms are shown below, as well as significant terms in the related field of military strategy. The selection is intended to illustrate different definitions, as well as different connotations of the same terms used in the literature of arms control and disarmament. The glossary is not exhaustive, but selective.

The terms defined have been taken from the *Arms Control and Disarmament Glossary* (Second Draft) of the Arms Control and Disarmament Agency, dated June 1965, and from the *Dictionary of United States Military Terms for Joint Usage* (Short Title: *JD*), The Joint Chiefs of Staff, Washington, D.C., dated 1 December 1964.

The draft glossary of the Arms Control and Disarmament Agency is an unpublished document; it does not represent official ACDA usage of the terms defined nor does it contain any stamp of approval by that agency. The glossary was intended to clarify concepts involved in terms in frequent and common use by government personnel and others interested in arms control and disarmament matters. As such the compilation of terms and their definitions should be taken as preliminary and subject to further refinement.

It will be noted that the Arms Control and Disarmament Agency draft glossary frequently contains definitions taken from the JD of the Joint Chiefs of Staff. In those instances where the Arms Control and Disarmament Agency differs from the JD or where the Joint Chiefs of Staff have defined a term not used by the Arms Control and Disarmament Agency, the abbreviation JCS has been used to indicate usage by the Joint Chiefs of Staff.

ARMS CONTROL. *ACDA.* (1) Any plan, arrangement, or process, resting upon explicit or implicit international agreement, governing any aspect of the following—the numbers, types, and performance characteristics of weapon systems (including their *command and control,* logistics support arrangements, and any related intelligence-gathering mechanisms) and the numerical strength, organization, equipment, deployment, or employment of the armed forces retained by the parties (it encompasses *disarmament*) (JD); (2) on some occasions, those measures taken for the purpose of reducing instability in the military environment (JD); (3) all the forms of military cooperation between potential enemies in the interest of reducing the likelihood of war, its scope and violence if it occurs, and the political and economic costs of being prepared for it (Schelling and Halperin).

Variations: The wise management of arms by nations to enhance the safety of the international environment against accidental, unintended war and war resulting from strategic miscalculation. Also may refer to the development of more discriminating military capabilities.

ARMS CONTROL AGREEMENT. *ACDA.* The written or unwritten embodiment of the acceptance of one or more arms control measures by two or more nations (JD).

ARMS RACE. *ACDA.* A reciprocal build-up in the quality or quantity of the military power of two opponents, caused by each striving to maintain or achieve a desired military posture relative to the other (RS/RAND); the competitive and cumulative proliferation or accretion of weapons (or increase in their destructive power) or the build-up of armed forces, based upon conviction on the part of each of two national adversaries that only by trying to stay ahead in military power can it avoid ultimate failure of its foreign policy (WEC/IDA).

BALANCE. *ACDA.* (a) Adjustments of armed forces and armaments to the end that one state does not have military advantages vis-à-vis other states agreeing to the measure; (b) internal adjustments by one state of its forces to the end that it can cope with all aspects of remaining threats to its security in the post arms control agreement era (WEC/JD).

BALANCE OF POWER. *ACDA.* An equilibrium or adjustment of power (as between potentially opposing sovereign states) such that no one state is willing or able to upset the equilibrium by

Note: Terms marked *ACDA* are not official definitions of the Agency.

waging war or interfering with the independence of other states
(Webster); an actual state of affairs in which power is distributed
among several nations with approximate equality (Morgenthau).

Variations: A concept of military power relationship that assures
attainment or maintenance of key national objectives, e.g., deterrence of general war, even though forces of two or more states
are unequal, *or,* on the other hand, a concept of power relationship
that evens out forces, say through disarmament measures, removing
inequalities in comparative military strength and by this or other
means reduces instabilities. Concept may more appropriately be
applied to alliances rather than individual states.

BALANCED FORCES.

Variations: Elements of force(s) complementary to each other.
Implies ratio of the various elements is such that the force is best
constituted to execute its assigned mission effectively and efficiently.

Land, sea, and air forces kept substantially equal in terms of
their size or expenditures of money.

COMMAND. *JCS.*

1. The authority vested in an individual of the armed
forces for the direction, coordination, and control of military forces.
2. An order given by a commander; that is, the will of the commander expressed for the purpose of bringing about a particular
action. 3. A unit or units, an organization, or an area under the
command of one individual. 4. To dominate by a field of weapon
fire or by observation from a superior position.

CONTROL. *ACDA.*

Supervision of the implementation of *arms control*
or *disarmament* agreement to provide assurance that it is being
observed by all parties (RS). Note: This is the sense in which
control has been used by both sides in the disarmament negotiations since 1955. Webster defines *control* as "power or authority
to guide or manage, directing or restraining domination," but
control means *verification* in French and Russian.

JCS. Authority which may be less than full command exercised
by a commander over part of the activities of subordinate or other
organizations.

CONTROLLED RESPONSE. *JCS.*

The selection from a wide variety
of feasible options of the one which will provide the specific
military response most advantageous in the circumstances.

Note: Terms marked *ACDA* are not official definitions of the Agency.

COMMAND AND CONTROL. *ACDA.* (1) An arrangement of personnel, facilities, and the means for information, acquisition, processing, and dissemination employed by a commander in planning, directing, and controlling operations (JD); (2) a mechanism with the following major tasks; (a) to collect and evaluate data relevant to the operation of military forces, (b) to transmit orders and information to military forces, and (c) possibly, to serve as a communication link with an enemy before or after the onset of open hostilities (RAND).

Variations: The differences in the definition of terms "command," "control," and "command and control" presented here are intended to illustrate the need for precision in the use of terms defining authority, e.g., for peacekeeping/armed forces under arms control/disarmament agreements. The meaning of various terms used in this field, say in their implications regarding residual national rights, are often misleading or obscure.

COUNTER-DETERRENCE. *ACDA.* The neutralization of an adversary's ability to deter certain action which one might wish to take; the policy of neutralizing an adversary's policy of deterrence (IDA).

COUNTERFORCE. *ACDA.* The employment of strategic air and missile forces in an effort to destroy or render impotent selected military capabilities of an enemy force under any of the circumstances by which hostilities may be initiated (JD).

Variations: Primary usage of the word "counterforce" refers to employment only of strategic offensive forces. When reference is to use of both strategic offensive and defensive forces, the word "damage limiting" is now considered more appropriate. ("Counterforce" is or can be a "damage limiting" measure.) The concepts of "counterforce" and "damage limiting" should be distinguished from so-called "city sparing" strategies, which call for attacks only against military objectives, while reducing collateral damage, e.g., to the population in cities, as much as is feasible to attain objectives. The purpose is hopefully to discourage enemy attacks on one's own cities.

COUNTERVALUE STRIKE. *ACDA.* A military assault against targets thought to be of great value to the enemy, regardless of their value to the attacker, e.g., an attack against population centers

Note: Terms marked *ACDA* are not official definitions of the Agency.

(RS/WEC/RAND). Sometimes called *countereconomy, counter-city* (TEMPO).

DAMAGE-LIMITING. *ACDA.* Use of strategic forces to reduce the capacity of the country being attacked to inflict damage on the attacker, i.e., a *counterforce attack* (WEC).

Variations: Reduction of potential enemy capabilities to inflict damage on population/industrial targets through destruction of his offensive weapon systems. The reduction of enemy capabilities may include both strategic offensive and defensive weapon systems.

DELIBERATE, FLEXIBLE RESPONSE. *ACDA.* Action taken by a decision-maker with sufficient information and time to understand the consequences; action taken by a person capable of choosing the timing, targets, and scope (RS/SRI).

Variations: Also referred to as "deliberate selective" and "controlled flexible" response.

DETERRENCE. *ACDA.* The prevention from action by fear of the consequences. Deterrence is a state of mind brought about by the existence of a credible threat of unacceptable counter action (JD).

Variations: The term is often used without an adjective, when the user intends minimum, mutual or graduated deterrence, or active, counter, denial, extended, passive, or other sub-categories of deterrence. (See *minimum, mutual, graduated, counter-deterrence.*)

DISARMAMENT. *ACDA.* Reduction of military forces or armaments, especially to levels set by international agreement (RS).

JCS. The reduction of a military establishment to some level set by international agreement.

ESCALATION. *ACDA.* The deliberate or unpremeditated increase in the scope or violence of a war (RAND); the growth of a small conflict into a broader and more violent one by successive but non-deliberate steps (Hadley); ascension up a ladder of conflict levels (WEC).

JCS. An increase in scope or violence of a conflict, deliberate or unpremeditated.

Note: Terms marked *ACDA* are not official definitions of the Agency.

Variations: Deliberate increase in the level of violence of military operations or scope of military commitment in an active confrontation or military campaign between states or in a war or equivalent.

Whether the escalatory step is deliberate or unpremeditated is a source of ambiguity. A more fundamental ambiguity, however, is what change in the level or scope of conflict represents escalation (escalation to what). The word may be used for any increase in military commitments or operations that increase the risk of general nuclear war, i.e., whatever in the enemy's view involves a major change of strategic purpose, as when moving from counter-insurgency to local war, or local war to general war.

FLEXIBLE RESPONSE. *ACDA.* The capability to react across the entire spectrum of possible challenge, for coping with anything from general atomic war to infiltration and aggressions such as threatened Laos and Berlin in 1959 (IDA); the capability of military forces for effective reaction to any enemy threat or attack with actions appropriate and adaptable to the circumstances existing (JD).

Variation: Effective reaction capability at any level of conflict or confrontation.

FORWARD STRATEGY.

Variations: Defense at the perimeter of confrontation, e.g., between East and West Germany's borders, not in depth in the heartland of the area to be defended, e.g., Western Europe.

Defense through projection of forces to key strategic points on the globe, i.e., with base rights and friendly allies, equipped with military forces capable of supporting a global power's requirements.

GENERAL AND COMPLETE DISARMAMENT (GCD). *ACDA.* Reduction of armed forces and armaments by all states to levels required for internal security and for an international peace force (JD); a program to insure that states will have at their disposal only those non-nuclear armaments, forces, facilities, and establishments as are agreed to be necessary to maintain internal order and protect the personal security of citizens; and that states shall support and provide agreed manpower for a United Nations peace force (JSAP).

Note: Terms marked *ACDA* are not official definitions of the Agency.

JCS. Reductions of armed forces and armaments by all states to levels required for internal security and for an international peace force. Connotation is "total disarmament" by all states.

Variations: Adding the concept of international peace force to the concept of GCD is not accepted by all states, e.g., the Soviet Union. The term GCD may refer to a general objective of policy characterized by agreed, phased reduction of armed forces of all states under appropriate levels of inspection and control, not altering the established relationship of forces or relative military power of states.

Alternately, the expression may reflect a strategy in support of "peaceful coexistence," the Communist strategy of protracted conflict.

It may be used as a concept to promote pacifistic objectives or to reduce the strength of world powers relative to weaker states. (See *arms control.*)

GENERAL PURPOSE FORCES.

Variations: Forces designed to have a broad range of capabilities in contradistinction to strategic forces which are designed for a paramount purpose, with capabilities for other missions distinctly secondary thereto. Forces designed, developed, produced or deployed for wars at lower levels of violence than general nuclear war; thus, forces designed primarily for counterinsurgency, local and limited wars, and theater support of general war operations are called general purpose forces. Some or all general purpose forces, e.g., those employed in a theater of operation that may be used directly against an enemy's frontal and operational forces in zones of combat, may also be referred to as "tactical forces."

GRADUATED AND RECIPROCATED INITIATIVES IN TENSION REDUCTION (GRIT). *ACDA.* A program of unilateral initiatives for reducing international tensions and bringing about eventual disarmament, proposed by Dr. Charles E. Osgood (TEMPO).

GRADUATED ACCESS INSPECTION. *ACDA.* Nationwide inspection in which the types of activities inspected, the inspection techniques, and the rights of the inspectors are expanded in accordance with the progress of disarmament (ST).

Note: Terms marked *ACDA* are not official definitions of the Agency.

GRADUATED DETERRENCE. *ACDA.* Deterrence of an enemy from carrying out a provocative venture by causing him to fear that this might be countered by acts leading to non-central war consequences, such as *limited war* or economic reprisal, which on balance would render the contemplated venture unprofitable (RAND); a policy aimed at preventing aggression by threatening retaliation proportional to the offense, generally applied to the threat of nuclear retaliation, esp. with tactical weapons, in case of aggression (RS/IDA).

INSPECTION. *ACDA.* Agreed procedures by which individuals either as representatives of national states or international organizations conduct activities for the primary purpose of verifying compliance with arms control and disarmament agreements (Woods Hole Summer Study). See also *control, verification.*
JCS. In arms control, the physical process of determining compliance with arms control measures.

Variations: The application of all measures of an international or other arms control/disarmament authority to ascertain compliance with agreements, checking for evidence of non-compliance. The meaning of the word comprehends a broad spectrum of techniques, time phasing, targets of inspection, political purposes, and scope. Some meanings actually might be better defined by such terms as "limited surveillance," "pro forma investigation" and the like. The term "policing" rather than "monitor" is usually used when the reference is to inspection by a formal international control organization. The term can also be used as a form of or equivalent to intelligence. (See *verification, graduated access inspection, progressive inspection,* and *zonal inspection.*)

INVULNERABILITY. *ACDA.* Condition that exists when, regardless of the scale and timing of his attack, an aggressor cannot expect to destroy a target (ST). This may be achieved by a combination of military measures, e.g., hardening of installations, active defense of these installations, and mobility and dispersal of forces (TEMPO).

Variations: The concept of invulnerability used in conjunction with retaliation has led to the development of the concept of invulnerable second strike force. This refers to offensive nuclear strike forces that cannot be effectively destroyed or neutralized in a first strike, preemptive, or blunting attack, because of active defenses, hardening, dispersal, concealment, or mobility, and which

Note: Terms marked *ACDA* are not official definitions of the Agency.

can therefore be fired in a second strike against an aggressor initiating a nuclear attack. Term is to be contrasted with "preemptive"
or "first strike" forces, that is, forces which, because of their
vulnerability to enemy fire, must be fired/launched before the
enemy attack (or before arrival of enemy warheads on target) to
be effectively utilized. Context may relate invulnerable force to
stability; vulnerable force to instability.

MILITARY STRATEGY. *ACDA.* The art and science of employing
the armed forces of a nation to secure the objectives of national
policy by the application of force, or the threat of force (JD).

Variations: The art of planning, developing, and using armed
forces, in peace and war, to support national objectives. (See
strategy.)

MINIMUM DETERRENCE. *ACDA.* A doctrine based on the belief
that total nuclear war would inevitably result in mutual suicide
(RS/TEMPO). Therefore there is little need for a *counterforce*
strike capability and reliance would be placed upon a relatively
small invulnerable retaliatory force (ST). Hence, a finite level of
reliable nuclear capability could be determined which would be
capable of such population casualties that the adversary would be
deterred from provoking such a response (WEC). Sometimes
called *finite deterrence* (TEMPO).

Variations: Term may be used as equivalent or similar to the
concept of "nuclear umbrella," in some purely deterrent contexts.
Distinctions arise in usage between "minimum" and "finite"
deterrence; the latter may refer to a lower level of capability.

MUTUAL DETERRENCE. *ACDA.* The situation that obtains between
two powers when each is deterred from attacking the other (i.e.,
launching a *first strike*) because the damage expected to result
from the victim's retaliation *(second strike)* would be unacceptable; usually thought of as applying only to attacks upon the
homelands of the opponents, but sometimes extended to important
interests and commitments outside the homelands (IDA).

MUTUAL EXAMPLES. *ACDA.* Parallel, unagreed reductions of forces,
armaments, or expenditures by opposing sides, e.g., the American
and Soviet budget reduction of 1963-64 (RS).

Note: Terms marked *ACDA* are not official definitions of the Agency.

Variations: Regulation or prohibition of military-technological activities by means of informal, tacit moves (also called "reciprocal measures"). Alternately the term may be considered as a variant of unilateral disarmament (no inspection or verification), if the other side does not reciprocate or the action of the other side does not correspond to the action of the initiating state in regard to a particular capability, inventory, force, policy, or measure.

Nth COUNTRY. *ACDA.* The next country of a series to acquire nuclear weapons (IDA).

JCS. A reference to additions to the group of powers possessing nuclear weapons—the next country of a series to acquire nuclear powers.

Variations: A reference to countries not possessing nuclear weapons or advanced weapons (military equivalent to underdeveloped countries). Part of nuclear power tactics is or may be to suppress or prevent competition from weaker states (insured hegemony) or to avoid additional threats of uncontrolled risks of military involvement in conflicts between lesser powers. (See *proliferation.*)
Sometimes referred to as the "fourth-country problem" prior to the time France became a nuclear power.

NUCLEAR-FREE ZONES. *ACDA.* Areas in which the production and stationing of nuclear weapons would be prohibited (RS).

Variations: A variant of neutralization on a regional basis; an aspect of polycentrism; a strategy to reduce Western/Soviet influence in contended areas or to alter regional power relationships.

NUCLEAR PARITY. *ACDA.* A mutually recognized equivalence of nuclear military power between two adversary states such that the military plans of both are based upon qualitatively similar though not quantitatively identical factors of strength. Generally employed with primary reference to the correlation of strategic power (IDA). See also *nuclear saturation, parity.*

JCS. A condition at a given point in time when opposing forces possess nuclear offensive and defensive systems approximately equal in over-all combat effectiveness.

NUCLEAR SATURATION. *ACDA.* The point where, although one power is stronger than the other—perhaps much stronger—both

---

Note: Terms marked *ACDA* are not official definitions of the Agency.

are capable of inflicting crippling or quasi-mortal injury on the other (Churchill).

Variations: The idea that as stockpiles of nuclear weapons increase, a point is reached beyond which further increases add little or nothing to a nation's deterrence or war-making capabilities. When the saturation point has been reached neither side can attain a superior or decisive capability over the other.

NUCLEAR SHARING. *ACDA.* A policy whereby a major nuclear power gives nuclear weapons to an ally while retaining a veto right over the use of the weapons (IDA).

Variations: A policy of controlled proliferation under international/multinational military and/or political authorities with or without veto retention partly to obstruct independent proliferation (an expression equivalent to proliferation). The question of veto is not necessary to the definition.

NUCLEAR SUPERIORITY. *ACDA.* (1) Advantage possessed by a side having a nuclear striking force so large that it would be credible that its possessor might use a nuclear strike in retaliation to conventional aggression and still have sufficient nuclear capability to carry out a *second-strike* response (RS/WEC/TEMPO); (2) situation in which one side in a strategic confrontation possesses a greater number of strategic delivery systems (ST).

Variations: Size of forces is not considered the primary factor by many authorities but force capability, nuclear warheads, or megatonnage, or deliverable nuclear fire are held to be essential.

PARITY. *ACDA.* The quality or state of being equal; close equivalence or resemblance; equality of rank, nature, or value; likeness (Webster). Numerical equality between Western and Communist nations in an international conference or organization (RS).

Variations: Parity is the same as equality. Variations concern whether the measure is in real terms of recognized power and what is to be measured, for example, whether the reference should be to parity/equality in firepower, number of delivery/launch vehicles, or parity/equality in regard to percentage of civilian casualties that can be inflicted or percentage of industrial capacity (or MVA) that can be destroyed. Equality (or parity) can be calculated as a static, pre-conflict relationship, in terms of gaming

Note: Terms marked *ACDA* are not official definitions of the Agency.

war scenarios, or in cold war power terms, that is, related or *not* related to the effectiveness of political applications. (See *nuclear saturation.*)

PEACEKEEPING. *ACDA.* Term applied to institutions or measures for the maintenance of peace and the peaceful settlement of international disputes (RS).

Variation: A military force established under and controlled by an international institution, the purpose of which is to prevent or stop military conflicts between small powers that could involve major nuclear powers (and thus cause risks of general nuclear war).

PROGRESSIVE INSPECTION. *ACDA.* A system in which the intensity and scope of inspection increases with the progress of disarmament (ST).

PROLIFERATION OF NUCLEAR WEAPONS. *ACDA.* The acquisition of national nuclear capabilities by states not previously possessing them, either by the dissemination by nuclear powers of weapons or information necessary for their manufacture, or by the development of domestic nuclear programs (RS).

STABILITY. *ACDA.* (1) An international situation in which there are inherent forces that tend to combat disruptive influences or to restore order whenever disruptive developments threaten it (IDA); (2) an international political and military situation in which the loss to a potential aggressor would be greater than the gain, so that aggression does not occur (ST).

Variations: A mutual relationship of nuclear deterrence (power equilibrium), characterized by mutual constraint on military initiatives because of risks of unwanted conflict escalation.

A condition of balance or other relationship of forces that reduces international tensions (regardless of numerical force relationships).

A policy of avoidance of military programs that will cause potential enemy "to accelerate the arms race."

STRATEGIC ADVANTAGE. *ACDA.* The over-all relative power relationship of opponents which enables one nation or group of

---

Note: Terms marked *ACDA* are not official definitions of the Agency.

nations effectively to control the course of a military/political situation (JD).

Variations: Advantage a major power may possess in regard to the most likely outcome of a strategic nuclear weapons exchange, *or,* advantage as to the credible image of strategic nuclear power that may serve as a backdrop to the pursuit of foreign policy objectives.

STRATEGIC FORCES.

Variations: Forces designed, developed, produced, or deployed to have the capability of long-range attack against global powers, against their nuclear attack forces, cities and other targets related to general war fighting and sustaining capabilities, *or,* forces capable of supporting military and political operations at *all* levels of conflict and confrontation, characterized by capabilities to launch an operation from outside the immediate area of conflict or confrontation.

Forces capable of performing vital, independent military missions, which can affect the outcome of a campaign or war or the attainment of a major objective of foreign policy. The effects of such operations on the enemy's military forces may be both short- and long-term.

STRATEGIC MISSION. *ACDA.* A mission directed against one or more of a selected series of enemy targets with the purpose of progressive destruction and disintegration of the enemy's war-making capacity and his will to make war. As opposed to *tactical* operations, *strategic* operations are designed to have a long-range, rather than immediate, effect on the enemy and his military forces (JD).

STRATEGY. *ACDA.* The art and science of developing and using political, economic, psychological, and military forces as necessary during peace and war, to afford the maximum support to policies, in order to increase the probabilities and favorable consequences of victory and to lessen the chances of defeat (JD).

UNACCEPTABLE DAMAGE. *ACDA.* Degree of destruction anticipated from an enemy *second strike,* sufficient to deter a nuclear power from launching a *first strike* (RS).

Note: Terms marked *ACDA* are not official definitions of the Agency.

Variations: The level of assumed damage an enemy can be expected to inflict on a state's homeland in a nuclear exchange which would influence the leadership of a state to avoid the risks of general war. Unacceptable damage may be estimated in terms of percentage or amount of the economic/cultural base and/or population that the state attacked can destroy/kill in a second strike. There is no exact measure of these values.

The term may also be applied to assumed levels of residual physical/human resources required for the restoration of the society after an attack. It may also be applied to lower levels of conflict, in comparisons between a state's objectives in a military conflict and the expected price in damage received that might be paid to attain them.

VERIFICATION. *ACDA.* The totality of means, of which inspection is just one, by which one nation can determine whether another nation is complying with obligations under an arms control or disarmament agreement (Woods Hole Summer Study). The act or process of verifying or the state of being verified; the authentication of truth or accuracy by such means as facts, statements, citations, measurements, or attendant circumstances; the procedure required for the establishment of the truth or falsity of a statement (Webster). Any action ascertaining that agreed measures are in fact being taken and the provisions complied with by the parties to the agreement (IDA).

JCS. In arms control, any action, including inspection, detection and identification, taken to ascertain compliance with agreed measures.

Variations: The meaning of the terms "inspection" and "verification" overlap. "Verification" is a more comprehensive term and refers more to monitoring activities by national as opposed to international means but may refer to both together. To the Communists the word "verification" is more limited than "inspection"—more international in objective and more restricted as to means and frequency. (See *inspection.*)

VIOLATION.

Variation: A demonstratively provable breach or infringement of a treaty or agreement, accepted as such by an offended state or control organization, causing lapse of constraining provisions or abrogation of the treaty or agreement.

Note: Terms marked *ACDA* are not official definitions of the Agency.

ZONAL INSPECTION. *ACDA.* (1) Inspection that is initially limited to particular geographic areas within a country (ST);
(2) plan proposed by Louis Sohn in which each cut in armaments would be accompanied by an extension of controls to a
specified part of the nation's territory. Each nation would be
divided into zones at the beginning of a disarmament program,
and inspection would be gradually extended to additional zones
as disarmament proceeded (TEMPO/RS).

ABBREVIATIONS

ACDA—United States Arms Control and Disarmament Agency, *Arms
Control and Disarmament Glossary* (Second Draft), June 1965.

Hadley—Arthur T. Hadley, *The Nation's Safety and Arms Control.*
New York, 1961.

IDA—Institute for Defense Analyses. "Lexicon of Terms Relevant to
National Security Studies on Arms and Arms Control," in *Proceedings
of the Seminar on Deterrence and Arms Control.* Washington, 1960.

JD—Joint Chiefs of Staff. *Dictionary of U.S. Military Terms for Joint
Usage.* Washington, 1964.

JSAP—U.S.-U.S.S.R. Joint Statement of Agreed Principles, September
20, 1961.

JCS—Joint Chiefs of Staff. *Dictionary of U.S. Military Terms for
Joint Usage.* Washington, 1964.

RAND—RAND Corporation. *Glossary of Terms on National Security.*
RM-2754. Santa Monica, 1961.

RS—ACDA Reference Research Staff.

SRI—Stanford Research Institute. *U.S. Unilateral Arms Control Measures and the Setting for Disarmament Negotiations.* n.d.

ST—ACDA Science and Technology Bureau.

TEMPO—TEMPO Technical Program, General Electric Company.
*Arms Control Guide: An Annotated Bibliography with Glossary, Direc-
tory, Biographies, and Research.* Santa Barbara, 1963.

Webster—*Webster's New International Dictionary of the English
Language.* Third edition. Springfield, 1961.

WEC—ACDA Weapons Evaluation and Control Bureau.

Note: Terms marked *ACDA* are not official definitions of the Agency.

INDEX